630

P9-DTL-628

L. A. HILL

WORD POWER 3000

Vocabulary Tests and Exercises in American English

Tokyo
Oxford University Press
Hong Kong   Singapore

Oxford University Press

Oxford   New York
Athens   Auckland   Bangkok   Bombay
Calcutta   Cape Town   Dar es Salaam   Delhi
Florence   Hong Kong   Istanbul   Karachi
Kuala Lumpur   Madras   Madrid   Melbourne
Mexico City   Nairobi   Paris   Singapore
Taipei   Tokyo   Toronto

and associated companies in
Berlin   Ibadan

OXFORD and OXFORD ENGLISH are trade marks of
Oxford University Press.

© Oxford University Press (Tokyo) 1982

All rights reserved. No part of this publication may be reproduced,
stored in a retrieval system, or transmitted, in any form or by any means,
without the prior permission in writing of Oxford University Press.

This book is sold subject to the condition that it shall not, by way
of trade or otherwise, be lent, re-sold, hired out or otherwise circulated
without the publisher's prior consent in any form of binding or cover
other than that in which it is published and without a similar condition
including this condition being imposed on the subsequent purchaser.

ISBN 0-19-581897-0

Illustrated by Miho Miyazaki

Printing (last digit):
40 39 38 37 36 35 34 33 32 31

Printed in Japan
by Tokyo Art Printing Co., Ltd.
Published by Oxford University Press K.K.
2-4-8 Kanamecho, Toshima-ku
Tokyo 171

Contents

Introduction

This is the second of a series of three books in American English whose purpose is to help students build up their English vocabulary. Particular attention has been paid to college entrance requirements. The first book uses a vocabulary of 1500 words, the second takes the student from there up to a vocabulary of approximately 3000 words, and the third adds another 1500, to bring the total up to 4500.

Each book contains six blocks of work, which can be used at regular intervals throughout the school year. In *Word Power 3000* each block consists of the following varieties of exercise: Pictures, Synonyms, Opposites, Derivatives, Words in Sentences, and, to round off, Prepositions and Adverbial Particles.

It will be noticed that "content" words are generally practiced only once, while prepositions and adverbial particles are often practiced several times. The aim here is to reinforce understanding of items whose meanings and uses are both complex and fundamental to the study of English.

There is always one correct answer except in some cases in Synonyms and Opposites. Here, alternative answers are sometimes available. Such cases help to alert students to subtle shades of similarity and difference. The separately available Answer Keys give example sentences for contextualization.

The word list at the end of the book contains all the words practiced in the exercises. In addition to the new items, this list includes all those words presented in *Word Power 1500* and reused here. (The latter are marked with (*1500*).)

As in *Word Power 1500*, British English variants are shown along with the American English forms that are used in the exercises.

strap. hay. sack. thorn. thumb. tune. snatch. lord
clay. creep. sew(sewn) sow(sown) stalk whisper wither

PART 1

Pictures

Look at the pictures and complete the sentences with the correct word from the parentheses:

1

This man is putting down a _trap_ (catch, strap, trap, trip) to catch rabbits. He is putting it near some _hay_ (hate, hay, high, shy). He has a _sack_ (box, sack, sock, stock) beside him. The young tree on the left is covered with sharp _thorns_ (thorns, thumbs, tunes, turns). You can see a _spider_ (fly, spider, spin, support), and there is a _snake_ (snake, snatch, warm, worm) in the grass.

2

This is a _load_ (load, lord, road, weight) of corn. It is on its way to the _mill_ (mile, mill, mind, mine) to be made into flour. There was a good _crop_ (clay, crab, creep, crop) in this field this year. It was _sown_ (sewn, shown, soon, sown) last January. Now the _stalks_ (stalks, stakes, sticks, stocks) are long, and the corn is ripe. The weather is so hot and dry that the leaves on the plants on the left have _withered_ (killed, whispered, withdrawn, withered).

1

bull. dock donkey hedge dave deer licking drain
stumble stump poultry poverty peck scatter scratch

3

The animal in the middle of this picture is a __bull__ (ball, bear, bell, bull). The one on the left is a __donkey__ (dock, donkey, horse, monkey), and the ones on the other side of the __hedge__ (edge, heads, hedge, huge) are __deer__ (dare, dear, deer, donkey, sheep). The mother is __licking__ (licking, liking, locking, rocking) the young one.

4

This is an open place in some __woods__ (wood, wooden land, wood land, woods). A man is __splitting__ (speaking, spitting, splitting, supplying) a __log__ (load, lock, log, rock) with an ax, and a horse is __dragging__ (digging, dragging, draining, drugging) a tree __stump__ (stamp, stuff, stumble, stump) out of the ground. It has a lot of __roots__ (loads, roads, roots, routes).

5

These birds are different kinds of __poultry__ (policy, poultry, poverty, powerfully). The chicken on the right is __pecking__ (eating, packing, pecking, picking) another chicken. It has pulled one of its __feathers__ (fathers, feathers, figures, further) out. Another chicken is __scratching__ (catching, clapping, scattering, scratching) the ground to find bits of corn, and another has found a __worm__ (warm, whom, worm, wound) and is going to eat it.

2

haste sacred weave wipe paws whip bark whistle
porter strip vessel liner linger cape bury wreck
anchor

1 Pictures PART 1

6

This is a ____ (donkey man, haste man, horseman, house man). He is sitting in his ____ (sacred, sadder, saddle, sadness) and holding a ____ (weave, whip, whisper, wipe). One of his dogs is ____ (backing, bargaining, barking, shouting), and another is licking one of its ____ (hands, pairs, paws, pays). The ground is very ____ (dusty, mad, muddy, murder). Another dog is running away, and the man is ____ (whipping, whispering, whistling, withering) to call it back.

7

The woman on the right is ____ (an air principal, a stewardess, a waiter, a waitress). She is wearing a ____ (dress, uniform, union, universal). The man on the left is a ____ (part, port, porter, poultry). He is pushing a ____ (bag, back, trick, trunk) which has a ____ (stamp, stop, strap, strip) around it. The ____ (handbag, handful, handle, hand) is broken.

8

There are several ____ (boats, ships, vessels, whispers) here. One of them is a ____ (line, liner, linger, lion). It is in the middle of the ____ (bay, boy, by, cape). There are some others in the ____ (decks, docks, dogs, ducks). On the left, you can see the ____ (deck, dock, dog, duck) of a half-buried fishing boat which was ____ (locked, rocked, waked, wrecked) here many years ago. Near the fishing boat, there is an old ____ (anchor, anger, angle, anxious).

3

2 Synonyms

Put a circle around the word or words on the right which mean about the same as the word on the left. (If more than one answer is correct, mark *all* the correct ones.)

1 absence *lack*   (lack) lock, luck, present
2 absolute *complete*   complete, quite, stupid, thorough
3 accustomed to *used to*   agreed, attacked, received, used to
4 ache *pain*   ever, field, pain, same
5 action *deed 行為*   busy, deed, film star, real
6 actual *real*   busy, doing, film star, real
7 amount *quantity*   funny, hill, quantity, weapon
8 anger *rage fury 狂怒*   every year, fury, rage, worry
9 area *district*   district, living, quarrel, zone 帶, 區域
10 argue *quarrelling*   bend, district, order, quarrel 吵架
11 attach *tie*   fight, like, tie, try
12 attempt *try*   attract, tie, try, watch
13 beg *plead*   large, plead, sack, want
14 being *creature*   asking, creature, having, take
15 besides *also*   also, edges, middles, near
16 bother *trouble*   edge, sister, trouble, two
17 boundary *border*   border, edge, parcel, sure
18 breeze *light wind*   have children, kindly, light wind, very cold
19 brief *short*   be sure, short, sorrow, take in air
20 capable *able*   able, a lot, catch, hat
21 capture *catch*   able, catch, chief, rug
22 chatter *talk*   break, shine, talk, type
23 commence *begin start*   begin, rule, start, trade
24 conceal *hide*   advise, concern, hide, join
25 condition *state*   agreeing, fighting, going on, state

3 Opposites

Put a circle around the word or words on the right which have about the opposite meaning of the word on the left. (If more than one answer is correct, mark *all* the correct ones.)

(handwritten: go ashore, to the shore, ge down, onto a ship vehicle, passenger)

1 aboard — onto a ship (passenger vehicle) →to the shore → ge down   below, ashore, alight, underneath
2 admit ⟷ deny   be sorry, deny, prove, victory
3 adopt ⟷ reject   keep out, reject, rejoice, retreat
4 advance ⟷ ritire   reject, rejoice, retire, retreat
5 affection ⟷ hate   halt, hate, hunt, interest
6 ahead ⟷ behind (fondness)   aboard, abroad, behind, below
7 altogether ⟷ partly   alone, lonely, partly, separately
8 ancient ⟷ modern   calm, happiness, moderate, modern
9 apart ⟷ together   all, altogether, together, whole
10 appear ⟷ disappear   disagreeable, disappear, disappoint, reject
11 appoint ⟷ dismiss   area, be late, dismay, dismiss — discharge
12 arrest ⟷ release   descent, latest, release, relief — to set free
13 backward ⟷ forward   forward, front, politeness, modern
14 bare ⟷ covered   clothes, covered, coward, wine
15 base ⟷ top   bottom, lie, stop, top
16 beneath ⟷ above   above, beside, overhead, under
17 beyond ⟷ this side of   hated, loose, this side of, united
18 birth ⟷ death   above, dead, deaf, death
19 blush ⟷ go pale   dirty, go pale, red, tree
20 brief ⟷ long   die, long, short, vegetable
21 broad ⟷ narrow   arrow, narrow, near, wide
22 calm ⟷ restless   go, restless, result, stupid
23 calm ⟷ distress, disturb   distinct, distress, district, disturb {3}
24 capture ⟷ release   free, not able, release, sailor
25 cause ⟷ result, effect   bless, effect, reject, result

4 Derivatives

Complete these sentences with words which have the same root as the word in *italics*:

1 A word was *omitted* [leave out] from the cable by mistake, and this _omission_ [電報] has confused us all.

2 After the accident there was *blood* everywhere. A man was _bleeding_ from a bad cut on his leg.

3 After the terrible heat, the cool weather was like *heaven*. .... Yes, it was _heavenly_, wasn't it?

4 A lot of Old Tokyo was *destroyed* in an earthquake. After its _destruction_, stronger buildings were put up.

5 Although Joan's young, she shows a lot of good *sense*. And her brother's very _sensible_ too. [賢い]

6 Are you *hungry*? ... _Hunger_ is the least of my problems at the moment.

7 I suppose Jenny's *jealous* because her little brother got so many presents. .... Not really, _jealousy_ isn't a big problem with her.

8 Before the people leave the church, the priest *blesses* them, and they go out soon after this _blessing_ [祝福]

9 Can you *add* the names of your students to this list? .... Yes, and in _addition_, I can give you the ones in Mary's class, and some _additional_ ones from last year.

10 Can you *prove* that Bill did it? .... No, I have no real _proof_

11 Can you *suggest* what I should do next? All _suggestions_ will be welcome.

12 Is Harding Construction Company going to *undertake* the subway project? .... I doubt that small company could handle such an _undertaking_.

13 Dave's a *strong* boy. He has a lot of _strength_ in his arms, and he's _strengthened_ his legs, too, by running a lot.

14 Did the arrangements *satisfy* you? .... Yes, I was very _satisfied_, and everything was done to Mary's _satisfaction_ too. .... I found it all very _satisfactory_ also. [罰する]

15 Was Joe *punished* for breaking the window? .... Yes, his _punishment_ was to stay behind after the other children went home.

16 Did they *treat* you well at the hospital? .... Yes, they were very kind, and the medical _treatment_ was very good, too.

17 Did you *slip* on the floor? I'm afraid it's very _slippery_

4 Derivatives  PART 1

18 Does anyone in your family *act* on the stage? .... Yes, Martin is a professional _actor_, and I think Linda will be a good _actress_ when she's older.

19 Does Bob go out *hunting*? .... Yes, he's a keen _hunter_

20 Do ghosts *exist*? .... Well, there are some people who believe in their _existence_ 存在；实体

21 Do you *employ* a lot of people? .... Yes, we're quite big _employers_. We have over 1000 _employees_ 雇佣对象

22 Do you *intend* to stay here? .... Yes, that's my _intention_ 意向

23 Do you live in the *center* of town? .... Yes, I live in _central_ Boston.

24 Eskimos *inhabit* the northern parts of America. In many places they are the only permanent _inhabitants_ 有住的；定居者

25 Roger Carter has been *appointed* principal of our school. His _appointment_ was announced yesterday. 任命；委任

26 George is a good *judge* of character, but in this case I think his _judgment_ is too harsh.

27 Some of the most *famous* people in the world never really wanted _fame_ n. 名声 at all.

28 Henry's *lost* a lot of money during the past year, but it's the _loss_ of his wife that's affected him most. _loose_ n.（丢失、损失）

29 Jim has *offended* me. .... Well, you shouldn't take _offense_ so easily.

30 Has your son been *admitted* to Yale? .... I don't know, I haven't seen the list of _admissions_ yet.

first offense 初犯

5 Words in Sentences

Complete these sentences with the correct word from the column on the right:

1 Africa used to be called the Dark _Continent_ because so little of it was known to Europeans.

Contest, Continent, Continual, Continue

2 After eating all those green apples, Jim got a bad _stomachache_

ache stomach, middle pain, stomachache, stumble ache

3 After eating his bread and jam, Martin's fingers and face were very _sticky_

glue, sticky, stiff, stock

4 After Linda's wedding, her father made a few polite _remarks_ about her new husband's family.

marks, remarks, remedies, reminds

5 After our soup and meat, we were given a sponge _pudding_

public, pudding, pulling, putting

6 After the accident, the driver managed to _stagger_ to the nearest house and call an ambulance.

flatter, flutter, stage, stagger

7 "Do you _deny_ robbing the bank?" the judge asked the prisoner.

agree to, describe, deny, allow

8 After no rain for several years, there was _famine_ in parts of northeast India.

fame, familiar, family, famine

9 After we'd been talking for twenty minutes, there was a short _pause_ during which nobody spoke.

pass, pause, paws, pious

10 After we'd run for a quarter of a mile, I could hear George _panting_ behind me.

painting, panning, panting, pointing

11 After winning the cup, our team came home in _triumph_

fame, genius, success, triumph

12 Our school has a PTA. That's the Parent-Teacher _Association_

Association, Astonishment, Attention, Situation

13 All the workers in our factory belong to the same _union_

joint, together, union, unite

14 A lot of buildings were destroyed by a _major_ earthquake in Tokyo in 1923.

magic, major, mayor, mere

15 Americans often have fried eggs and _bacon_ for breakfast. (成）   bacon, baker, baking, banker

16 There have been animals for millions of years, but _human_ beings like us have a short history.   human, humble, humming, humor

17 Four hundred years ago few people spoke English, but now it's used _throughout_ throughout the world.   across, out of, throat, throughout

18 Are your students good at English? .... They _vary_ a lot. Some are good, and others are not.   change, distinguish, doubt, vary

19 As our ship was about to leave, we went _aboard_ quickly.   a board, aboard, abroad, ahead

20 At the end of the year's work, we _reviewed_ returned, revealed, reviewed, everything we'd learned.   repaired

21 Be careful! We're going to hit the shore! Try to _steer_ the boat straight.   stare, steer, still, stir

22 Be careful when you go on the beach. The _tide_ is out right now, but when it comes in, it comes very fast.   tide, tied, tight, wave

23 Before Peter went to Japan, he asked his bank to _transfer_ some money to Tokyo for him.   carry, fetch, transfer, transport

24 Before you buy that cloth, _examine_ ___ it carefully.   accent, accustom, examine, example

25 Before I decide what to do, I have to _consult_ with my partners.   concert, consult, insult, result

26 Before they start work, salesmen need a lot of ____.   actions, business, draining, training

27 Before you're allowed to drive, you have to get a driver's _training_.   card, text, license, liking

28 Before you can measure distances on a map, you have to know the _scale_ of the map.   scale, scar, skill, successful

29 Before you can travel anywhere abroad, you'll have to get a _passport_   passport, pastime, visa, wiser

30 Before you go to the United States, you'll have to get a _visa_ in your passport.   entrance, let, visa, vision

PART 1 5 Words in Sentences

31 Brighton, in England, is a very popular holiday _resort_   report, resort, result, retire

32 Can you hear the piano? Someone's playing a _tune_   music, note, tune, turn

33 Children like putting a lot of _jam_ on their bread.   jaw, jewel, jam, additional

34 Christians believe that after death, there is _eternal_ life.   attention, eternal, intention, interior

35 Climbing that mountain was an interesting new _experience_ for me.   expense, expensive, experience, expert

36 Columbus discovered America in 1492, but the first real European _settlement_ there was not till seventeen years later.   secretary, separate, settlement, sufficient

37 Come on! Say something! You aren't _dumb_, are you?   dam, damp, drum, dumb

38 David died last week. His _funeral_ will be tomorrow.   bury, funeral, furnace, furnish

39 Did Jenny say anything about her sister? …. No, she didn't _mention_ her at all.   medicine, mend, mention, minister

40 Did you fly from New York to Tokyo _direct_, or stop on the way?   delicate, diary, direct, director

41 Don't drive so fast. There's a speed _limit_ here, you know!   end, limit, link, remedy

42 Don't leave that iron in the water, or it'll _rust_   loss, rest, rush, rust

43 Don't lend John anything: I don't _trust_ him.   breathe, relieve, trust, truth

44 Don't put so much in your mouth, or you'll _choke_   choke, joke, shake, shock

45 Do you want a soft pencil, or a hard one? …. Neither. I want a _medium_ one.   madam, media, medium, midday

46 Each state is divided into _counties_   counties, countries, counts, cousins

47 Eleven pounds is about the same as five _kilograms_   grams, kilograms, kilometers, centimeters

48 England is separated from France by the English _channel_

Chairman, Champion, Channel, Shallow

49 Mary's got _charm_. Everyone likes her.

charge, charm, seam, shame

50 Everyone in college likes Helen. She's the most _popular_ girl in the whole place.

like, peculiar, popular, population

51 Everyone was talking quietly, but when the teacher came in, the _hum_ of conversation stopped.

ham, hum, human, whom

52 Every Sunday, the church bells _waken_ us at 7:30 in the morning.

arise, open, rise, waken

53 Every time Ted sells a car, his company pays him a _commission_

commercial, commission, committee, wage

54 Five miles is nearly the same as eight _kilometers_

kill meters, kilograms, kilometers, lengths

55 From our living room, a narrow _passage_ leads to the hall.

pass, passage, passport, pastime

56 David had a very good job in the Middle East, but he came home for the _sake_ of his children's education.

sack, sacred, sake, silk

57 Joe is a truck driver. His hourly _wage_ is very high.

dollar, bread, salary, wage

58 Tim's gone to see Ellen, but I don't know for what _purpose_

perpetual, personal, purple, purpose

59 Tom doesn't have his own home yet. He lives in a _boarding_ house.

boarding, logging, border, board

60 Paul's retired now. He's the _former_ manager of our bank.

farmer, foaming, forever, former

61 George's house is small, but there's lots of _space_ in the roof to add more rooms.

source, space, spice, suppose

62 Joe's out of the hospital now and getting more _active_ again.

action, active, actor, actual

63 Dave's always dreaming. He isn't a very _practical_ person.

practical, practice, produce, product

64 Bob is angry because he's lost some money. .... Oh, I saw he was in a bad _temper_ but I didn't know the reason.

temper, temple, temptation, thunder

65 Robert and Tom went through a lot of dangers together. They were close *companion*.

companies, companions, complaints, compliments

66 Peter's at the State College now. He's *Professor* of English there.

Popular, Prisoner, Professor, Progress

67 Tim's long illness *affected* his performance in the examinations a lot.

accepted, affected, afforded, effected

68 Robert speaks English with a German *accent*, because he's lived in Germany all his life.

accent, accept, accident, extent

69 Tim thought he wasn't good enough to take the examination, but I *urged* him to try.

edged, staggered, swore, urged

70 Bill very seldom goes to the park on Saturdays. He _____ goes to the river to fish. *Mostly*

morally, mortally, most, mostly

6 Prepositions and Adverbial Particles

Complete these sentences with the correct word from the column on the right:

1 _In_ the absence of the Principal, Mr. Jones is in charge of the school. At, By, In, To

2 According _to_ Larry, the weather has been beautiful in Miami. at, for, to, with

3 I've never been accused _of_ coming to work late, I'm glad to say. at, of, to, with

4 Are you accustomed _to_ heat, or does it make you tired? at, of, to, with

5 The medicine acts _on_ the brain. at, on, to, towards

6 _In_ (1) addition _to_ (2) all my other work, I now have to do the accounts. (1) At, In, On, With
(2) from, of, to, with

7 We've decided to admit Tom _to_ our club. at, by, for, to

8 Japan is _in_ (1) advance _of_ (2) most other countries in making cars. (1) at, in, on, with
(2) at, from, of, on

9 Sally has a big advantage _over_ most girls when it comes to games because she's so tall. above, on, over, with

10 I'm amazed _at_ how much English your son already speaks. at, in, of, on

11 You should never speak _in_ anger to a small child. at, for, in, on

12 Helen is very anxious _about_ her mother's health. about, at, for, with

13 Apart _from_ this dictionary, I have no Japanese books. for, from, of, with

14 Our new garden is very Japanese _____ _in_ appearance. at, by, in, on

15 You had better apply _to_ (1) the manager _for_ (2) a job here. (1) at, in, on, to
(2) for, from, to, towards

16 Don't argue _with_ Joan. Just do what she says. at, on, to, with

17 Who's going to make arrangements _for_ Norah's wedding? for, from, of, to

13

18 You ought to be ashamed _of_ yourself, pushing that little boy over! — at, from, of, with

19 If you attach this rope _to_ that ring, we can pull your boat in. — in, on, to, upon

20 Pay attention _to_ what your teacher says! — at, in, on, to

21 David's an intelligent boy. He's also _above_ average in sports. — above, on, outside, over

22 Our dog barks _at_ strangers. — at, in, on, to

23 Please put this medicine _beyond_ the children's reach. It's dangerous. — at, beyond, by, from

24 Yuki is Japanese _by_ (1) birth, but American _by_ (2) marriage. — (1) at, by, of, with
(2) at, by, of, with

25 Mary gave birth _to_ a beautiful little girl this morning. — at, of, to, with

PART 2

1 Pictures

Look at the pictures and complete the sentences with the correct word from the parentheses:

1
The man on the right is a *gardener* (garden, gardener, generation, grain). He is *digging* (digging, dipping, dragging, scratching) with a *spade* (spade, spare, split, support). The man on the left is a *painter* (painter, pattern, porter, prayer).

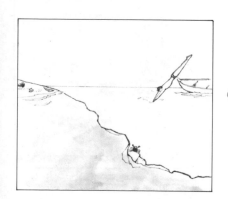

2
The *depth* (debt, deep, depth, length) of this water increases from left to right. There are some pretty *shells* (chairs, sells, sets, shells) on the beach, and there is a *crab* (clap, crab, crumb, spider) in the water. The man on the right is *diving* (diving, driving, dying, jumping) into the water from a boat.

dive

15

3

This is a _dam_ (dam, damp, dock, dumb). Its purpose is to control _floods_ (flatters, floods, flutters, frowns). The water _overflows_ (overcomes, overflows, overlooks, overthrows) down several _pipes_ (bites, papers, piles, pipes) into the _canal_ (can, canal, candle, candy) below. It is wet today, and the hills are _misty_ (miss, misty, must, fogged). Two boys have found _shelter_ (sharp, shelter, shield, shut) from the rain under a tree.

4

On the left of this picture there is a _cave_ (cage, cape, carve, cave). The _hillside_ (cliff, highway, hillside, hire) rises to a _ridge_ (lid, reader, rich, ridge) behind it, and on the right there is a _swamp_ (stamp, swallow, swamp, sword). It is a hot, _sunny_ (sandy, sun, sunny, sunrise) day, but it is _shady_ (sad, saddle, shady, shed) and cool inside the cave.

5

These boys are playing on a board at the _edge_ (age, corner, edge, hedge) of a field. The board is _balanced_ (balanced, blessed, branched, buzzed) on a _block_ (belong, black, block, brick) of wood. At the moment, the board is _level_ (leather, level, liberal, lively), and the boys are neither up nor down.

6

This triangle is made of metal _rods_ 杆
(loads, rays, roads, <u>rods</u>). The _length_
(breadth, length, long, width) of each is
80 centimeters, and the _height_ (breadth,
height, high, width) of the whole thing is
about 70 centimeters. The _angle_ (anchor,
anger, angle, bend) at the top is sixty
degrees (declares, degrees, diseases, zeros),
and the _area_ (air, area, ear, hair) of the
triangle is about 0.3 square meters.

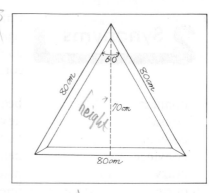

7

This store sells _jewelry_ (jealousy, jellies,
jewelry, joyful). The _jewel_ (jealous, jelly,
jewel, joy) in the ring in the middle is a
diamond (demand, diamond, dining, pearl).
The _earrings_ (air rings, earrings, hair rings,
hear rings) on the right have _pearls_ (pairs,
pearls, pears, peels) in them. The
<u>necklace</u> on the left is not made of real
stones. It is made of glass _beads_ (beads, 项链
beats, beds, birds). The woman in the
store is wearing a beautiful _fur_ (fair,
far, fear, fur) coat.

8

This store sells men's <u>clothes</u>. In the
middle there is an _overcoat_ (out coat,
overcoat, overhead, overthrow) for cold
weather, and on the right a _raincoat_
(rainbow, raincoat, rain goat, water
coat) for wet weather. On the left there is
a shirt with long _sleeves_ (slaves, sleeps,
sleeves, slippers). They have _cuffs_
(coughs, cows, cuffs, curves) at the ends
of them. The man is taking some _banknotes_
(material, property, payments, bank-
notes) out of his pocket because he has
decided to buy the shirt.

2 Synonyms

Put a circle around the word or words on the right which mean about the same as the word on the left. (If more than one answer is correct, mark *all* the correct ones.)

1 connect ~join~ — beat, fight, join, persuade
2 consider ~think about~ — advise, a lot, build, think about
3 content ~satisfied~ — be filled with, fight, satisfied, suit
4 convince ~persuade~ — belief, persuade, suit, talk
5 crazy ~mad~ — mad, mud, noisy, swear
6 (curse) ~swear~ — interested, line, mad, swear
7 deadly ~fatal~ — fatal, heaven, hell, not alive
8 declare ~state~ — go bad, go slow, help, state
9 demand ~ask~ — ask, devil, part, deny
10 department ~bureau~ — store, bureau, going away, home
11 deserve — give, merit, offer, want
12 (desire) ~wish~ — dry land, wish, merit, scorn
13 despise ~hate~ — look at, lose hope, hate, want
14 determine ~decide~ — decide, end, stop, study
15 disease ~illness sickness~ — illness, not comfortable, sickness, unhappy
16 display ~show~ — make angry, not play, refuse, show
17 distant ~remote~ — different, how far, remote, trouble
18 (distinct) ~clear~ — area, belief, clear, far
19 (eager) ~enthusiastic~ — big bird, gain, enthusiastic, interesting
20 earnest ~serious~ — gain, least difficult, richest, serious
21 endless ~infinite~ — infinite, last, perpetual, straight
22 enormous ~huge~ — hard work, huge, unusual, worried
23 entire ~whole~ — ask, come in, last, whole
24 (evident) ~clear~ — clear, escape, proof, wicked
25 evil ~wicked~ — at all times, be at home, clear, wicked

desiretogirlfriend

3 Opposites

Put a circle around the word or words on the right which have about the opposite meaning of the word on the left. (If more than one answer is correct, mark *all* the correct ones.)

1 certain ⟷ uncertain — uncertain, unexpected, unfortunate, unusual
2 civil ⟷ military — military, millimeter, minister, square
3 coarse ⟷ fine — bless, file, fine, result
4 common ⟷ rare, scarce — go away, rare, real, scarce
5 crooked ⟷ straight — bare, raw, silent, straight
6 cunning ⟷ sincere — similar, since, sincere, singer
7 dare ⟷ be afraid — able to hear, be afraid, hated, light
8 defeat ⟷ victory, win — victim, victory, win, wind
9 defend ⟷ attack — able to hear, attach, attack, win
10 delicate ⟷ rough — bitter, nasty, raw, rough
11 delicious ⟷ horrible — horrible, horror, hurried, rough
12 deposit ⟷ withdraw — rise, shallow, withdraw, wither
13 difficulty ⟷ ease — ease, easily, easy, same
14 agreeable ⟷ disagreeable, unpleasant — disagreeable, unpleasant, enemy, impatient
15 display ⟷ hide — height, hide, play, please
16 domestic ⟷ foreign — folly, foreign, horrible, safe
17 doubt ⟷ be sure — be sure, light, single, upwards
18 downward ⟷ upward — crossword, sunrise, upright, upward
19 downwards ⟷ upwards — praise, sure, upstairs, upwards
20 dreadful ⟷ excellent, wonderful — empty, excellent, interesting, wonderful
21 drunk ⟷ sober — empty, medicine, sober, water
22 dull ⟷ interesting, lovely — after, giant, interesting, lively
23 eastern ⟷ western — difficulty, drunk, northern, western
24 elsewhere ⟷ here — here, nowhere, other, somewhere
25 evil ⟷ good — God, good, hidden, never

19

PART 2 — 4 Derivatives

4 Derivatives

Complete these sentences with words which have the same root as the word in *italics*:

1 Have you *applied* for a place at Harvard? .... Yes, I sent in my _application_ last week.

2 Have you *arranged* to take a vacation in Mexico? .... Yes, all the _arrangements_ are made.

3 Have you *informed* Helen about the new arrivals? .... Yes, I sent her the _information_ yesterday.

4 Have you *paid* for your house yet? .... I've made the first _payment_

5 Have you *solved* the puzzle yet? .... No, but I think I've nearly found the _solution_

6 Ellen has a *marvelous* voice. .... Yes, and you can only _marvel_ at the way she plays the piano too.

7 Laura is very *anxious* about her children's health, and her _anxiety_ makes her protect them too much.

8 She *performed* that dance beautifully. .... Yes, her whole _performance_ has been marvellous.

9 Arlene's condition has *improved*, and it looks as if this _improvement_ is going to continue.

10 Sue *sleeps* a lot. She always feels _sleepy_ after meals.

11 Stephanie thanked us *warmly* for our help. But of course she has always been a _warm_ person. .... Yes, that's what I like about her — her _warmth_

12 How are you going to *defend* yourself? .... Well, I believe that attack is the best form of _defense_

13 How are you going to *transport* these goods? .... The store arranges the _transport_

14 Animals always *protect* their young until the young ones can look after themselves and _protection_ is no longer necessary.

15 You saw the robbers, so please *describe* them. .... Well, I think those _descriptions_ in the newspaper were about right.

16 How do young Americans *greet* their friends? .... These days, the usual _greeting_ is just "Hi."

17 How do you *pronounce* this word? .... I'm sorry, I don't know the _pronunciation_ either.

20

18 Try to make *friends* wherever you can. _Friendship_ is a marvelous thing.
19 I *admire* Nancy very much. .... Yes, I've nothing but _admiration_ for her too.
20 I *advised* Larry to get a new job. .... Yes, that was my _advice_ to him too.
21 I believe in setting wild birds *free* if they are caged. _freedom_ is the best gift we can give them.
22 I can't *use* a pen like this. It's completely _useless_ to me.
23 How much do you *weigh*? .... Oh, I haven't checked my _weight_ for years.
24 I don't mind what people *believe* as long as they don't force their _beliefs_ on others.
25 If I could *choose* between these dresses, my first _choice_ would be the red one.
26 I find it difficult to *breathe* in all this smoke. Whenever I take a _breath_, it hurts.
27 If it isn't *convenient* for you to come tomorrow, please arrange another date at your _convenience_.
28 We're going to exchange our *electric* stove for a gas one. The problem is that _electricity_ is getting too expensive.
29 They believe that if you have enough *faith*, you can do wonderful things. They believe that God helps _faithful_ people.
30 My hands used to be *soft* and smooth, but not any more. .... You'd better use this cream. That'll _soften_ them.

5 Words in Sentences

Complete these sentences with the correct word from the column on the right:

1 George wants $1000 for his old car, but I don't think it's _worth_ as much as that.

price, valuable, value, worth

2 Tim won the 100-meter event, so he's the new _champion_

champion, channel, sandwich, sharpen

3 Hong Kong isn't independent. It's still a British _colony_

collection, colony, column, owner

4 Harry started painting twenty years ago, and now he's very _successful_

considerable, succeeded, success, successful

5 Frank escaped from prison by _disguising_ himself as a priest.

discovering, discussion, disgracing, disguising

6 Many animals claim _terr_ and fight to keep other animals away.

land, stripe, territory, throughout

7 Tom isn't rich and can't _afford_ a new car every year.

affect, afford, effect, effort

8 Have you seen today's newspaper? There's an interesting _article_ about Japan.

alcohol, annual, article, artistic

9 Having a fever means that your _____ is too high. _temperature_

hot, temper, temperature, temptation

10 Helen cleaned the table until there wasn't a _grain_ of dust on it.

grain, grand, gray, grew

11 Susan didn't want to stop and eat lunch with Linda, but Linda _insisted_

increased, insisted, instructed, interested

12 Helen is always forgetting things. For _example_, yesterday she left her purse at the store.

accent, case, examine, example

13 Mandy's a clever girl. She loves doing _puzzles_, and she always gets the answers.

persuades, pursues, pursuits, puzzles

14 The old man usually hated children, but for some reason he took a _liking_ to Mark.

happiness, lighting, like, liking

15 Helen loves to study, and she does all her schoolwork with _enthusiasm_

enormous, entertain, enthusiasm, interior

16 My aunt's rich. She owns a lot of _property_ preparation, properly,
in the middle of our town. property, prosperity

17 A lot of Chinese live in that _district_ of distance, distant, distinct,
San Francisco. district

18 She saves money by doing all her _washing_ bathing, showering, soaping,
at home. washing

19 Jane's extremely intelligent. In fact, I generous, generation, genius,
think she's a _genius_ gentle

20 Barbara's wedding was a big _occasion_ action, exchange, occasion,
There were more than two hundred occasional
guests.

21 Cinderella left the Prince at the _stroke_ blow, stretch, stroke, struck
of midnight.

22 You've won this fight, but I'll get my return, revenge, review,
revenge next time we meet! winning

23 The men at the factory are paid their pay, salaries, wages, ways
wages every week.

24 The church is always full when people plead, please, preach,
know that Father Peter's going to _preach_ precious
there.

25 Henry's been killed, and the police say marveled, multiplied,
he was _murdered_ murdered, muttered

26 Here's a list of the _goods_ we stock in goats, god, good, goods
our store.

27 Here's a cable which needs an _immediate_ immature, immediate,
answer. immortal, impatient

28 Here's your coffee. Would you like clean, climb, cream, crime
cream?

29 How are your English classes? .... Oh, progress, propose,
I've made a lot of _progress_ this year. prosperity, protest

30 How big's your garden? .... Half an ache, acre, each, eager
acre

31 How can George get the men to do authority, autumn, overhead,
what he says when he has no _authority_ governor

32 How should I go to Chicago? .... That defends, depends, descends,
depends on how fast you want to get hangs
there.

23

PART 2 — 5 Words in Sentences

33 How's Peter doing in business? I
   don't know. I don't know anything
   about his _affairs_

   affairs, affects, affords,
   afterwards

34 How tall are you? .... My _exact_ height
   is five foot eight and three quarter-
   inches.

   accent, accept, exact, extra

35 How wide is the desk? .... One _meter_

   meat, meet, meter,
   measurement

36 How wide is your dining room table?
   .... Eighty _centimeters_

   centers, centimeters,
   centuries, meters

37 I always take my _annual_ vacation in
   July.

   anchor, angle, animal,
   annual

38 I can't hear you. Stop _muttering_ and say
   what you want to say.

   marveling, multiplying,
   murdering, muttering

39 I can't see a thing in this forest. We'll
   have to wait till _daylight_ before we start.

   daylight, deadly, diary,
   sunset

40 I couldn't hear what the children were
   saying, because they were _whispering_

   talking, whipping,
   whispering, wishing

41 I didn't actually tell John the answers
   to the questions, but I gave him several
   hints to help him.

   hinders, hints, hits, hunts

42 I don't just want the work done my
   way or your way. I want it done to our
   mutual satisfaction.

   both, metal, mutter, mutual

43 I don't know what you think of
   George's work, but in my _opinion_, it's
   very good.

   omission, opening, opinion,
   oppression

44 I don't like driving in New York, as it
   involves too much slow driving in heavy
   traffic.

   invents, invites, involves,
   values

45 I don't like John. His _continual_ complaints,
   day after day, make me angry.

   contain, content, continual,
   continuous

46 I don't like winter much. In _fact_ I
   really hate it.

   face, fact, factory, true

47 I don't mind where we go. Let's just
   wander about the park for a while.

   travel, voyage, wander,
   wonder

48 I don't think Mr. Williams is in his
   office, but I'll go and _check_

   check, cheek, chalk, shake

24

5 Words in Sentences PART 2

49 I don't trust that man at all. I think he's _plotting_ with his colleagues to take over the company.

plotting, plowing, purchasing profiting

50 I don't wear those narrow shoes, although I know they're the latest _fashion_

fashion, fasten, modern, mood

51 Don't be _deceived_ by appearances. Judith is much older than she looks.

deceived, decided, received, reserved

52 I heard a _shot_, and then three men came running out of the bank.

shock, shoot, shot, spot

53 If the bread's stale, _toast_ it, and then eat it with butter while it's still hot.

rest, test, toast, trust

54 If there's another world war, it may mean the end of _mankind_

kind man, mankind, meantime, meanwhile

55 If you found that money in the street, the _moral_ thing to do would be to take it to the police.

moral, more, moreover, mortal

56 If you listened to Peter, you'd think he was the best ball player in the world. .... Yes, he _boasts_ a lot.

boasts, boats, boots, posts

57 If you _multiply_ five by ten, you get fifty.

dive, divide, machinery, multiply

58 If you mix red and blue paint, you get _purple_.

people, purchases, purple, purpose

59 If you open a tank of airplane gasoline, a _vapor_ comes up out of it which you can't see.

dust, liquid, steam, vapor

60 If your brother or sister has a daughter, she's your _niece_

aunt, nephew, niece, uncle

61 If your feet ache, try putting some of this _powder_ on them.

dust, pour, powder, power

62 If you take your dog to the public park, you have to keep it under _control_.

central, continual, control, power

63 If you try long enough, you're _bound_ to succeed.

band, bomb, bone, bound

64 Your bag is in the lost and found. You'd better go and _claim_ it.

claim, climb, cream, crime

65 If you want that meat to taste good, you'd better add some _spice_

space, speaker, spice, spider

25

PART 2 | 5 Words in Sentences

66 If you want to buy an old car, I can tell you the name of a used-car _dealer_ not far from here.

daily, dealer, deal man, dearer

67 If you want to keep that meat for a long time, you'll have to _freeze_ it.

cold, feast, free, freeze

68 If you want to stick that photograph in the album, I can give you some _glue_

globe, glow, glue, grew

69 A group of local companies _donated_ $50,000 to help the hospital.

donated, exported, licensed, refused

70 If you want your floors to shine, polish them with _wax_

glue, honey, tax, wax

6 Prepositions/Adverbial Particles PART 2

6 Prepositions and Adverbial Particles

Complete these sentences with the correct word from the column on the right:

1 Who's _to_ blame for all this trouble?   at, of, to, with

2 James boasts all the time _about_ his beautiful new boat.   at, from, over, about

3 I'm _out of_ breath. I've run all the way here.   beyond, off, out of, over

4 I can't tell you the whole story now, but _in_ brief, my parents aren't coming here this summer.   at, for, in, on

5 When Len heard that his dog had died, he burst _into_ tears.   at, into, of, to

6 I didn't know you were capable _of_ cooking such a wonderful meal.   for, of, to, with

7 Before you leave, you'd better make certain _of_ getting return tickets.   by, for, of, to

8 If you buy a bicycle, we'll give you a pump and a lamp free _of_ charge.   from, of, with, without

9 You'd better check up _on_ that man before you give him any money.   at, in, on, to

10 _Under_ no circumstances am I going to leave without you!   At, On, Under, With

11 Mrs. Harris has died, and six people now lay claim _to_ her house.   at, of, to, with

12 Who is _in_ (1) command _of_ (2) this ship?   (1) at, in, on, over (2) above, at, by, of

13 You can't compare Joe's house _with_ Helen's!   against, over, with, beside

14 Jim has begun to complain _of_ frequent headaches.   at, from, of, with

15 You can leave early today _on_ condition that you stay longer tomorrow.   by, on, over, with

16 Our house isn't finished yet. It's still _under_ construction.   at, below, on, under

17 The police here come _under_ (1) the control _of_ (2) the city.   (1) at, below, from, under (2) at, from, of, with

27

18 You can come and do the work any
time _at_ your own convenience.   at, in, on, with

19 It's going to rain today. I'm sure _of_
it.   at, by, of, with

20 I hate it when people are cruel _to_
animals.   at, for, on, to

21 Our house was robbed _in_ broad   on/in
daylight.   at, by, in, on

22 Are you still _in_ debt? .... Yes, I owe
Mr. Williams $50.   at, in, on, under

23 What can you say _in_ (1) defense
_of_ (2) your behavior last week?   (1) at, in, on, to
     (2) at, from, of, with

24 I didn't like my job at first, but _by_
degrees I got to enjoy it.   by, in, on, with

25 Please answer this letter _without_ delay.
It's very important.   against, out of, outside,
     without

in brief
be capable of
make certain of
free of charge
lay claim to
☆ in command of
compair ... with
complain of
☆ on condition that
☆ in defense of

PART 3

1 Pictures

Look at the pictures and complete the sentences with the correct word from the parentheses:

1

These are skirts. The one on the left has white ____ (dots, doubts, shots, spots) on it, and the one on the right has white and black ____ (stops, straps, strips, stripes), and a broad black ____ (border, bother, boundary, hedge) at the bottom. Between them, there is a ____ (stop, strap, strip, stripe) of cloth with a ____ (cannot, knee, knot, not) in the middle.

2

____ (Modern, Handle, Traditional, Accustomed) methods like these have become popular in the last few years. The woman on the left is ____ (spinning, spitting, stirring, surrounding) some ____ (rope, thread, threat, treat), and the one behind her is ____ (viewing, wearing, weaving, whipping) it into cloth. The woman on the right is ____ (falling, flooding, folding, frowning) the cloth up and then ____ (robbing, rubbing, whipping, wrapping) it up in ____ (bands, bankers, bundles, burials) to send away.

29

3

The woman on the left is wearing an
____ (anchor, appeal, apron, area)
around her waist. There is a big ____
(stain, stand, stem, stone) on it. She has
____ (boots, slices, slippers, slopes) on
her feet. The woman on the right has
just come in. She is wearing a ____ (scar,
scarf, scout, shock) around her neck,
because it is cold outside, and she is
carrying a ____ (handbag, handful,
handle, trunk).

4

This is an ____ (ache, acre, arch, each).
It is supported on two ____ (colonies,
colors, covers, columns). There are ____
(clocks, crabs, cracks, crashes) in the
____ (base, basin, bus, bush) of one of
them. Behind, there are the ____ (rails,
rains, ruins, runs) of a big building, with
several wide ____ (caps, cracks, gaps,
grips) in the walls.

5

These are ancient soldiers. They are
wearing ____ (armor, armies, hammer,
murder) to protect their bodies. The one
on the left is holding a ____ (shell,
shield, should, shower) in his left hand,
and a ____ (sore, sow, sword, word) in
his right. The other man has an ____ (ax,
edge, eggs, instrument) as his ____ (gun,
waken, weapon, wedding), but he is also
carrying some ____ (arose, arrows,
needles, yellows) on his back.

6

You can see a _tank_ ____ (tank, tax, thank, think) in the center of this picture. You can see the _flash_ (flash, flesh, frame, freeze) of its gun. Some soldiers are ____ (clapping, creeping, crippling, cropping) up to try to attack it. A _bomb_ (bomb, bone, born, broom) has just _burst_ (based, blessed, burst, buzzed) on the left, and something is burning on the right. You can see the _flame_ (firms, flames, foams, frames) and smoke.

7

This girl is a _singer_ ____ (sincere, singer, single woman, performance). The _band_ (band, entertainment, bank, musician, committee) is behind her. The man on the left is playing the ____ (temper, triumph, trumpet, trunk), and the man farthest away is playing the ____ (drums, dumbs, thumbs, trunks). The people on the right are the _audience_ ____ (audience, authority, avenue, enormous). They are _clapping_ (clapping, crippling, cropping, handling).

8

This is a big party, and some of the people are holding _balloons_ (balances, balloons, balls, bargains). The man on the left has a big, black ____ (beard, hair, mustache, musician). He is ____ _yawn_ (jawing, yawning, yelling, yielding) because he is tired. The man on the right is _kissing_ (cashing, cursing, kicking, kissing) his wife. He has a glass of _wine_ (vain, wind, wine, wink) in his hand.

PART 3 · 2 Synonyms

2 Synonyms

Put a circle around the word or words on the right which mean about the same as the word on the left. (If more than one answer is correct, mark *all* the correct ones.)

1 excellent — big interest, too much, very much, wonderful
2 exhausted — did, lived, very interested, very tired
3 extraordinary — more, remarkable, too much, unusual
4 fancy — custom, dangerous, imagine, desire
5 fasten ~tie~ — go quickly, make fat, speed, tie
6 feast 祈禱 festival — large meal, danger, earliest, festival
7 fever — high temperature, less, shape, wilder
8 final — better, last, very good, woman
9 freedom — liberal, liberty, library, lifetime
10 furious — covered with hair, fire, tables and chairs, very angry
11 generous 漫不知心 — liberal, liberty, very clever, wonderful
12 gift — pleasant, present, presented, raise
13 glitter sparkle — bigger, make a noise, slip, sparkle
14 gloomy — happy, moaning, sad, wide
15 grieve — mourn, present, say hello, seize
16 guard protect — land, lead, protect, wind
17 guide lead — fly, lead, protect, slip
18 halt stop — seize, speed, stop, strongly
19 harm hurt — hand, hurt, meat, strong
20 hereafter from now on — chief, great fear, terrible, from now on
21 heroic brave — brave, local, terrible, very quick
22 hire rent — borrow, further up, mount, rent
23 holy sacred — broken, completely, sacred, terrible
24 icy very cold — my, smooth, sweet, very cold
25 indicate show — angry, free, show, tell

32

3 Opposites

Put a circle around the word or words on the right which have about the opposite meaning of the word on the left. (If more than one answer is correct, mark *all* the correct ones.)

1 expected _unexpected_ foolish, included, refused, unexpected
2 export _import_ fool, game, hide, import
3 express _ordinary mail_ carriage, fast, ordinary mail, airmail
4 exterior _interior_ dull, interior, ordinary, terrible
5 extreme _average_ average, fool, moderate, terrible
6 faint _bright_ bright, cunning, doubt, real _faint-hearted_
7 false _true_ gentle, rises, slow, true _false-hearted_
8 familiar _strange_ food, grandfather, male, strange
9 female _male_ baby, later, male, strange
10 fierce _meek gentle_ brave, meek, gentle, second
11 folly _wisdom_ domestic, partly, wisdom, wise
12 forbid _allow permit_ allow, blame, calm, permit
13 formerly _now_ freely, now, urban, without shape
14 fortunate _unlucky unfortunate_ bad luck, unlucky, free, unfortunate
15 foul _pleasant_ against, get up, pass, pleasant _foul-mouthed_
16 frequent _occasional, rare_ occasional, prison, rare, real
17 fully _empty partly_ calm, empty, partly, smooth
18 gain _loss_ laugh, loose, loss, once
19 good-natured _nasty_ badly, nasty, strange, unusual
20 gradual _sudden_ saddle, sorry, sudden, without education
21 handsome _ugly_ empty, hungry, much, ugly
22 happiness _sadness_ impossible, saddle, sadness, sure
23 happy quiet, said, sat, unhappy
24 harsh _mild_ cow, deaf, kindness, mild
25 hell _heaven_ deaf, heaven, him, valley

4 Derivatives

Complete these sentences with words which have the same root as the word in *italics*:

1 If your pencil isn't *sharp*, ___ sharpen ___ it with this knife.

2 If you want to *complain* about what you've bought, go to the ___ complaints ___ Desk.

3 This *machine* looks very modern. .... Yes, we're proud to say this company's ___ machinery ___ is very up-to-date.

4 If you want to *inquire* about addresses, please go to the ___ (n.) Inquiry ___ Office.

5 If you want to send a *message* to Robert, our ___ messenger ___ can take it. He's going that way.

6 I *hate* rude people, and my ___ hatred ___ increases as I get older.

7 I *love* music. .... Yes, I'm a music ___ lover ___ too.

8 I love the *music* Ellen plays. .... Yes, she's a good ___ musician ___. And her children are all very ___ musical ___ too.

9 I'm going to *measure* this room. I need the ___ measurements ___ for a new carpet.

10 There's been no rain in East Africa for months. Millions of *thirsty* people and animals may soon die of ___ thirst ___.

11 I never give in to *threats*. When people ___ threaten ___ me, I say nothing, however ___ threatening ___ they become.

12 In some countries, the poor are *oppressed*, and sometimes this ___ oppression (n.) ___ leads to trouble.

13 Is Fiji *independent*? .... Yes, it got its ___ independence ___ in 1971.

14 George says he's an *important* man these days. .... His ___ importance ___ isn't as great as he pretends it is.

15 Is Arthur a *neighbor* of yours? .... Well, he lives somewhere in our ___ neighborhood ___. He lives on a ___ neighboring ___ street.

16 Is John good at *art*? .... Yes, he's a successful ___ artist ___, and his wife is very ___ artistic ___ too.

17 Isn't the sunset *beautiful*? .... Yes, its ___ beauty ___ takes my breath away.

18 I sometimes think George is *mad*, but his ___ madness ___ never seems to last long.

19 Is this frame made of *wood*? .... No, but that picture has a ___ wooden ___ frame.

20 It's very *dark* in this room. .... Yes, I ___ darkened ___ it by closing the curtains, because ___ darkness ___ is the best thing for my headache.

21 It's very *moist* today, isn't it? .... Yes, there's always a lot of ___ moisture ___ in the air at this time of the year.

22 I was really in *despair* when we missed our plane. .... Yes, I was feeling _desperate_ too.

23 It was *kind* of you to help us. I'll always remember your _kindness_.

24 It was *difficult* to get to town from our hotel, but that was nothing compared with the _difficulty_ of getting back at night.

25 I was very *relieved* when Joan came home safely, but my _relief_ didn't last long because she got sick the next day.

26 I'm sure you're going to make a *fortune* in business. .... Thank you very much. In fact, I've been very _fortunate_ so far.

27 Joe seems to be a very *intelligent* child. .... Yes, everyone in that family has a lot of _intelligence_.

28 John *collects* stamps. He has a beautiful _collection_.

29 Bill does everything in great *haste*. .... Yes, I've noticed how _hasty_ he is.

30 Bob doesn't always *behave* very well, and I hate rude _behavior_.

. the Complaints Desk
the Inquiry Office
. hatred
. threat - threaten - threatening
. a music lover
. in great haste
. in despair
. darken

5 Words in Sentences

Complete these sentences with the correct word from the column on the right:

1 If you want your letter to get there fast, you'd better send it _express_

expense, expert, express, export

2 I hadn't seen Peter for twenty years, and when we met he had changed so much that I hardly _recognized_ him.

recognized, recommended, reminded, revealed

3 I hate people who are always late for appointments, so I always try to be _punctual_ myself.

partly, possible, punctual, purple

4 I haven't decided whether to help Roger or not, but I'll give the matter some _thought_ and tell you what I've decided tomorrow.

idea, taught, thinking, thought

5 I have to go to the dentist, because I have a _decayed_ tooth.

decayed, deceived, declare, dictionary

6 I hit my big toe against a rock a few days ago, and it's still so _sore_ I can't walk properly.

shore, sore, sorrow, sort

7 I knew Helen must have hurt herself badly when I heard her _moan_.

mean, moan, moon, morning

8 Mrs. Johnson's very popular, and all her students have a great _regard_ for her.

record, regard, regret, reward

9 I like the colors of those shirts, but I don't like the _patterns_ very much. I think the flowers are too big.

partners, patience, patterns, payments

10 I'll have to owe you for these goods. I don't have any _cash_ on me at the moment.

case, cash, cause, coin

11 I'm going to have an orange. That's my _favorite_ fruit.

favorite, fearful, festival, love

12 I'm not collecting this money for myself. I'm going to give it all to _charity_

character, charity, chatter, sharpen

13 I'm not going out tonight, because I have a terrible _headache_

hat ache, headache, head hurt, head pain

5 Words in Sentences PART 3

14 I'm not going to have any lunch, I've got no _appetite_
apparent, appearance, appetite, application

15 I'm not sure who that girl is, but _according_ to John, she's a student.
according, account, accustomed, following

16 I'm writing George about our vacation and asking him for a _prompt_ answer, because I need to make plans very soon.
pretend, prompt, pump, purpose

17 I'm sorry, but my grandfather can't hear you unless you speak loudly. He's _deaf_
blind, dead, deaf, death

18 I'm sorry, but you can't take so many courses. It's against school _policy_
police, policy, polish, produce

19 In Britain, they still have _lords_ and ladies.
loads, loaves, lords, roads

20 These days, a singer has to work hard to build up his or her _image_
image, imagination, imagine, import

21 In some countries you often don't pay the price you're asked for something. Instead you _bargain_
barber, bargain, bark, beggar

22 In Japan, the husband earns the living, and the wife usually runs the _household_
horseman, hospital, household, house hole

23 In our zoo, they've managed to get some rare animals to _breed_
bleed, bread, breed, breathe

24 In some Arab countries, women wear a _veil_ to cover their faces when they go out.
handkerchief, veil, wall, wheel

25 In the examination last month, half the _candidates_ were successful.
cabbages, calendars, candidates, candle dates

26 Which _direction_ is the river from here? .... North.
description, direction, director, side

27 I often write my letters by hand and then give them to my _secretary_ to type.
separate, substance, secret, secretary

28 The dollar exchange rate isn't too _favorable_ just now. Let's change our money next week.
faithful, favor, favorable, favorite

29 Is Tom a captain? .... Yes, I think that's his _rank_
height, lack, rain, rank

37

PART 3 — 5 Words in Sentences

30 It's clear there's a strong _link_ between smoking and heart disease. — join, joint, link, ring

31 I think cruelty to children is the worst _crime_ of all. — clean, climb, cream, crime

32 I'm sorry. I can't _approve_ your request for more money. — appear, apply, approve, prove

33 Some states in the US _condemn_ people to death for murder. — command, condemn, except, excuse

34 I think there must be a fly in the room, because I can hear a _buzz_. — base, burst, bus, buzz

35 I think you're very clever, and I'm not just trying to _flatter_ you. — flat, flatter, flutter, frighten

36 It's a _tradition_ in our country to eat turkey on Thanksgiving. — course, trading, tradition, use

37 It's natural for children to _rebel_ against their parents when they're about sixteen. — rebel, refer, royal, rubber

38 It isn't always easy to understand a foreign joke, because different countries have different senses of _humor_. — funny, humble, humor, hunger

39 It's no use going to the airport yet. The plane isn't _due_ till 12:30. — do, due, owed, own

40 Please _compare_ these pictures. The small one is much better. — company, compare, complain, equal

41 I took my car to our local service station last Friday to have it washed and _waxed_. — shining, taxed, waxed, shone

42 It's a beautiful night. Let's go out and sit in the _moonlight_. — light moon, moon, moonlight, sunlight

43 It's dangerous to swim in this river. There's a very strong _current_ which can carry you away. — career, contract, current, curtain

44 It's neither very hot nor very cold where I live. In fact, we have a very good _climate_. — climate, climb, crime, weather

45 Before the exam I _refreshed_ my memory by reading some old notes. — refreshed, refused, rejected, repaired

38

5 Words in Sentences   PART 3

46 I wanted to play football this
afternoon, but I didn't have enough
energy after my big lunch.

energy, enormous, engineer,
    increase

47 I would never have met my wife if
fate hadn't brought us together quite
by chance.

fat, fatal, fate, fight

48 I wrote Paul yesterday and *enclosed* some
photographs with my letter.

closed, enclosed, encouraged,
    shut in

49 Some people believe in the *Devil*, as
well as in God. (=satan)

Devil, Divide, Double, Evil

50 Jimmy put salt in our sugar bowl
instead of sugar this morning.
He loves playing *tricks* on people.

tracks, tricks, trips, trucks

51 Joan is in the hospital. There are seven
other women in the *ward* she's in.

ward, warn, wood, word

52 Linda's quite a close *relative* of ours.
She's our cousin.

family, relative, relieve,
    reveal

53 Jill's putting on weight now, but when
she was young, she was *slim*.

salary, slim, slipper,
    surround

54 Marilyn's very popular at school, so
she finds lots of *playmates*

planets, players, play girls,
    playmates

55 Susan's beautiful. She has a lovely face
and a wonderful *figure*

figure, finger, firm, village

56 Sally was so frightened when the boys
jumped down from the tree that she
screamed loudly.

said, screamed, seemed,
    streamed

57 Joe's only seven, but he loves *adventure*.
He climbs rocks and trees and swims in
the river all the time.

addition, advance,
    advantage, adventure

58 Frank tries to do too much, and there's
a danger of his *overworking* and getting sick.

overflowing, overtaking,
    overthrowing, overworking

59 Martin paints pictures, but he doesn't
make his *living* that way. He works in a
big store.

life, live, lively, living

60 Tony would have forgotten the *reminded*
appointment if I hadn't *reminded* him.

regarded, remembered,
    reminded, rewarded

61 Do you have a pen? Good. Please
make a *note* of this number: 0523477.

net, nod, not, note

5 Words in Sentences

62 John can't swim yet, but if you're
   patient and _____ him, he'll soon learn.

carriage, encourage, increase,
   inquire

63 John deserves to do well. He's a very
   _____ young man.

indoors, industrious,
   industry, interrupt

64 Alex didn't like what his company
   wanted him to do, so he decided to
   _____ and get another job.

reserve, resign, reverse, risen

65 The doctors have just found a
   wonderful new _____ that will make Bill
   better.

drag, draw, drug, duck

66 John's in college now. He's getting an
   excellent _____.

addition, edition, education,
   explanation

67 Max has told me what the cable was
   about, but I haven't seen the _____ of
   it.

tax, test, text, writing

68 The man heated the iron till it _____
   red, and then hammered it into shape.

glared, glittered, glowed,
   glued

69 That boy's full of _____. You never
   know what kind of trick he'll play
   next.

dismiss, mischief, minority,
   uncertain

70 Jim's a funny boy, and his stories
   always _____ me.

aim, amaze, amuse,
   announce

6 Prepositions and Adverbial Particles

Complete these sentences with the correct word from the column on the right:

1 I take delight in walking along the shore.
   at, from, in, of

2 Good engineers are in demand now.
   at, in, on, under

3 The amount you have to pay depends on how long they've worked for you.
   at, from, on, in

4 Who's in (1) charge of (2) this office while the manager is away?
   (1) at, for, in, on
   (2) by, from, of, with

5 When Peter lost his ticket, he was in despair.
   at, in, on, under

6 Unless you really devote yourself to your studies, you won't pass your examinations.
   at, into, onto, to

7 Japanese books differ from ours in that they start at the other end.
   at, from, to, with

8 Start now, and if you find yourself in difficulties, I'll help.
   at, for, in, on

9 Can you distinguish between the French and the Italian flags?
   among, between, from, under

10 Helen is without doubt the cleverest student in the school.
   out of, outside, over, without

11 I'm sure that Ted's cough is due to smoking.
   at, from, of, to

12 After winning our last match, we're eager for the next one.
   at, for, of, to

13 Well, now that you've learned the rules of the game, we can start playing in earnest.
   at, in, on, with

14 I always feel at ease with Janet.
   at, in, on, with

15 When does the new law come into effect?
   at, in, into, on

16 Jim was born on Midsummer's Night.
   at, by, on, under

17 You can take many different courses —art and design, for example.
   at, by, for, with

41

18 You can have my bicycle ___in_(1)
exchange _for_(2) your carpet.

(1) at, in, on, with
(2) for, of, off, out of

19 There are a lot of animals still __in__
existence which are much older than
Man.

at, in, on, with

20 Do you like sports? …. _to_ a certain
extent. (range)

For, To, With, Within

21 Mary eats a lot of fruit. _In_ fact, she
almost lives on it.

As, For, In, On

22 My mother doesn't have much faith
_in_ doctors.

at, for, in, on

23 Are you familiar _with_ the plays of
Shakespeare? William

at, for, on, with

24 Young people's clothes go _out of_
fashion very quickly now. They seem
to change every month.

down, off, out of, outside

25 My father's always finding fault _with_
modern youth.

at, in, on, with

PART 4

Pictures

Look at the pictures and complete the sentences with the correct word from the parentheses:

1

This is a bar. The man in the middle is filling a _pitcher_ (cup, bottle, jar, pitcher) with _beer_ (bare, bear, beef, beer). You can see the _bubbles_ (balloons, bubbles, buckets, bundles) on top. It is overflowing a little and _dripping_ (dripping, driving, dropping, trembling) on the floor. The people on the left are _customers_ (audiences, considers, customers, listeners). They are waiting for their drinks.

2

These men are _bakers_ (backs, bacons, bakers, bankers). The one on the left is taking _loaves_ (leaves, loaves, lovers, loves) of bread out of the _oven_ (open, oven, over, owner). The man in the middle is putting a _lump_ (lamp, body, lump, slice) of _dough_ (flour, flowers, cookies, dough) on the _scales_ (scales, scars, schools, stale) to weigh it. The man on the right is making _cookies_ (cookers, bread, cookies, cooks).

43

PART 4 | 1 Pictures

3

This is a kitchen. The cook on the left is putting some meat in a _pan_ (box, pain, pan, pen), and he is going to _roast_ (boil, rest, roast, route) it in the oven. The cook in the middle is cutting up a _cabbage_ (cabbage, candidate, carpet, cottage), and the one next to him is _carving_ (caring, carving, caving, charming) some meat. The boy on the right is cutting up an _onion_ (onion, opening, opinion, union) for a _sauce_ (sauce, society, sock, water) which the cooks are going to make.

4

The man on the left is putting some _____ (bears, beliefs, berries, buries) into a machine which will press the _juice_ (jewels, juice, sauce, water) out of them. The man in the middle has a _handful_ (hand, handful, hard full, load) of nuts which he is going to _grind_ (glide, grade, grind, ground) down to a powder. The man on the right is _peeling_ (baring, paling, peeling, pulling) an orange, and the boy is _scraping_ (rubbing, scraping, scratching, strapping) some potatoes.

5

This woman is putting a _spoonful_ (fork full, knife full, plate full, spoonful) of sugar into an empty _teacup_ (cap, cup of tea, cup tea, teacup). The _teapot_ (coffee pot, pot tea, tea glass, teapot) is behind it, and there is a small _basin_ (base, basin, cup, pitcher) on the right. There is a _slice_ (cutting, loaf, slice, slight) of cake on a plate, and there are some _crumbs_ (clubs, crops, crowns, crumbs) beside it.

44

6

On the left is a piece of ____ *machinery* (machinery, magician, magnificent, mischief). It is a *furnace* (funeral, furious, furnace, furnish) for making steel. *Sparks* (Rays, Sparks, Speaks, Talks) are flying out and falling to the ground. On the right is a pile of old *ashes* (ashes, asks, atlases, flames). Nearer us there is a (forklift) truck. It has stopped, and a *worker* (waiter, welfare, worker, work) is checking the truck's *battery* (battery, beauty, berry, butter).

7

High up on the left is a country ____ *village* (apartment, cottage, hut, village). It *overlooks* (overflows, overlooks, overtakes, overthrows) a rocky valley, and the ground *slopes* (sleeps, slips, slopes, straps) down steeply. The *landscape* (escape, land escape, landscape, land and sight) on the other side of the valley is not very interesting. There are a few houses that look no bigger than *huts* (spots, huts, neighborhoods, hats). Beyond them, the land is not *cultivated* (cultivated, groaned, grown, employed), and it is dry and almost a *desert* (deserve, desire, desert, desperate).

8

This is a wide ____ *avenue* (appointment, audience, avenue, average). There is a covered *ditch* (dig, district, ditch, hole) beside it. A girl is *cycling* (circling, cycling, kicking, slicing) along, and a man on a *motorcycle* (cycle motor, machine cycle, motor circle, motorcycle) is *overtaking her* (overflowing her, overtaking her, overthrowing her, taking her over). There is a *bus stop* (bush shop, bus station, bus step, bus stop) on the right. It has been raining recently and you can see a *rainbow* (bow rain, rainbow, raincoat, rain boy) in the sky.

2 Synonyms

Put a circle around the word or words on the right which mean about the same as the word on the left. (If more than one answer is correct, mark *all* the correct ones.)

1 infant ~baby~ · · · · · baby, less important, soldier, tell
2 instant *moment* · · · · be rude, example, moment, teach
3 joyful *happy (occasion)* diamond, happy, sweet, talking a lot
4 likely *probable* · · · · loving, possible, probable, similar
5 likewise *also / too* · · · also, clever, loving, too
6 location *place* · · · · · place, position, rough, situation　好地方
7 magnificent *marvelous* magic, making, making bigger, marvelous
8 manufacture *make/produce* control, make, produce, wonderful 製(造)
9 marriage *wedding ceremony 式* weight, mayor, weed, wedding
10 material *substance/stuff* importance, ripe, stuff, substance
11 mercy *pity 仁慈* earn, only, news, pity
12 method *way/manner* iron, manner, news, way
13 (midday) *noon* dirty, gently, noon, no one
14 moreover *also / too* also, motion, too, too many
15 motion *movement* also, moreover, movement, reason
16 motive *reason* also, movement, reason, movie
17 naked *bare* bare, bear, beer, manufactured
18 naughty *bad* bad, bed, local, nothing
19 neat *tidy きちんとした* bad, tidy, tight, want
20 necessity *need* however, neat, need, not look after
21 nevertheless *however* frightened, however, more, quicker
22 numerous *many* much, many, numbers, never
23 object *protest against* behave well, crime, notice, protest
24 odd *strange* also, ancient, borrowed, strange
25 opening *hole* doing, hall, hole, whole

46

3 Opposites

Put a circle around the word or words on the right which have about the opposite meaning of the word on the left. (If more than one answer is correct, mark *all* the correct ones.)

1 hinder *help* help, herb, outside, partner
2 hollow *solid* evil, goodbye, solid, very high
3 horror *joy* goodbye, joy, nice, silence
4 humble *proud* animal, prayed, proud, sadness
5 increase *reduce* answer, leave out, reduce, refuse
6 include *leave out* leave out, outdoors, outside, reduce
7 inferior *superior to* limited, outwards, secret, superior
8 inner *outer/outward* outer, outward, over, tell
9 inward *outward* ought to, outward, retired, very long
10 inwards *outwards* outdoors, outside, outwards, silently
11 lighten *make heavier* dear, heavy, make heavier, mistake
12 linger *hurry* fatter, hatred, hurry, shorter
13 liquid *solid* hated, soil, sold, solid
14 load *unload* polite, quiet, street, unload
15 loose *tight/stiff/* (firm), (stiff), (tight), win
16 loss *profit* found, profit, proof, tight
17 luxury *poverty* bad luck, (poverty), powerful, treasure
18 major *minor* certainly, mine, minor, town man
19 majority *minority* country, military, minority, small town
20 master *slave* ma'am, minor, proud, slave
21 mature *immature* artistic, extreme, immature, not important
22 meek *fierce* break, fierce, pride, proud
23 modest *proud/vain* ancient, oldest, proud, vain
24 mortal *immortal* animal, evil, hotel, immortal
25 muddy *dry* dry, midnight, Sunday, wet

· We are all mortal.

4 Derivatives   Complete these sentences with words which have the same root as the word in *italics*:

1 John was always too *weak* with other people. In the end his ___*weakness*___ lost him his job.

2 Mike has a very *loud* voice. When he reads ___*aloud*___ to his children after they're in bed, you can hear him all over the house.

3 Paul's *absent* today. .... Yes, I noticed his ___*absence* (n.)___

4 The Directors are strongly *opposed* to the plan, and their ___*opposition*___ means that it cannot be carried out.

5 Steve's a *lucky* man: he's won again. I never seem to have such ___*luck*___

6 Tom soon *repented* of being so rude, but his ___*repentance*___ came too late.

7 John's really a very *solitary* person. He loves ___*solitude* (n.)___

8 Even as an old man Uncle Bruce was always full of *vigor*. I hope I'll be as ___*vigorous*___ when I'm older. (u.)

9 Jimmy was filled with *shame* at what he had done. .... Yes, I thought he looked ___*ashamed*___ of himself.

10 Bob was *indignant* when he heard what Sue had said, but I don't think his ___*indignation*___ was necessary.

11 On *commercial* TV they show ___*commercials*___ during programs.

12 Let us *pray*. First a ___*prayer*___ for the old and sick.

13 Look at that man *begging*. .... Yes, there are quite a lot of ___*beggars*___ here.

14 Look at your *dirty* shoes! Please don't bring ___*dirt*___ into the house.

15 My sister *devotes* all her time to her children. I hope they remember that ___*devotion*___ when they grow up.

16 Ann has a *comfortable* home, and Jenny lives in ___*comfort*___ too.

17 Barbara's absolutely *loyal* to her friends, but I'm not so sure of Helen's ___*loyalty*___

18 Her daughter's always very *polite*. .... Yes, I've noticed her ___*politeness*___ too.

19 Joan keeps on *imagining* that she's ill. .... Yes, she's got a very active ___*imagination*___

20 Shirley *knows* a lot about medicine. I'm always surprised at her ___*knowledge*___.

21 Jane looks just *like* her mother. .... Yes, they're very ___*alike*___, aren't they?

22 Ellen's beautiful voice *astonished* me. .... It filled me with ___*astonishment*___ too.

48

23 It takes a lot of *skill* to become a tightrope walker. That performer's
unusually _skillful_, isn't she?

24 What a *delightful* gift! I'm _delighted_ 使我很

25 Jenny's skill at tennis *amazes* me. .... Yes, it fills me with _amazement_ too.

26 Mr. Edwards is the general manager of a big *bank*. He's a well-known
banker (teach)

27 My father taught me to *observe* things carefully, and now I use my
powers of _observation_ a lot. An intelligent _observer_ can learn a lot that's useful.

28 The little girl's eyes were full of *fear*. She looked up _fearfully_, thinking her
father would hit her.

29 The West *consumes* too much oil, and we must learn to cut _consumption_

30 Our cat is very *curious* about everything, and its _curiosity_ sometimes gets it
into trouble. 好奇的 好奇心

· repented of
· a solitary person
· be full of vigor
  ashamed of myself
· live in comfort
  It fills me with ⟨ astonishment
                   amazement
  I'm delighted
· cut consumption
  — curious about

PART 4 5 Words in Sentences

5 Words in Sentences

Complete these sentences with the correct word from the column on the right:

1 Jim's lazy. He has a very bad _attitude_ toward work.

attention, attitude, attractive, authority

2 Peter's in the hospital. He was the _victim_ of a careless driver.

object, result, sacrifice, victim

3 John isn't afraid of anything. In fact, he's sometimes too _bold_ for his own safety.

ball, bold, bound, bowl

4 Tony's in the _navy_ now. His ship is on the way to South America.

native, naughty, navy, never

5 He said my hair looked beautiful. .... That was a nice _compliment_

company, complaint, complete, compliment

6 Frank's car hit a wall, but he was lucky and managed to _escape_ unharmed.

escape, escort, expense, export

7 My chin feels rough. I forgot to _shave_ this morning.

safe, save, scarf, shave

8 Dad's getting old. He's beginning to complain about everything the younger _generation_ does.

age, general, generation, generous

9 John doesn't have much money, but he usually _earns_ a bit during summer vacations.

earns, ears, earths, wins

10 Bill's wife is arriving today. .... Oh? I didn't _realize_ he was married.

realize, receive, release, relieve

11 Dick thinks I'm very funny. Whenever he sees me, he begins to _grin_

grand, green, grin, grind

12 Max would be a good manager, I think. He has a strong _character_

capture, charity, chatter, character

13 Gerry writes books. The _title_ of his last one was "The Brown Land."

design, remark, title, total

14 Less than half the people in Dad's office smoke now, so they've become the _minority_

majority, minority, minutes, moderately

50

5 Words in Sentences PART 4

15 Listen to your teacher. Unless you pay _attention_ to what she says, you won't learn.

application, attention, attitude, attraction

16 Look at that bird. It _glides_ down to the ground without moving its wings at all.

glides, glitters, grinds, guides

17 Look at that strange woman! .... It's rude to _stare_ at people, Helen!

see, stare, start, store

18 Look at those birds staying in one place in the air by _flutter_ their wings.

flattering, flowering, flowing, fluttering

19 Susan dances with such _grace_ that it's always a pleasure to watch her.

glass, grace, grass, guess

20 Mary goes to church every day. .... Oh? I didn't know she was as _pious_ as that.

pious, possess, sacred, sacrifice

21 Martha has cooked for many years, so she's _expert_ at it.

accent, expect, expert, export

22 Ann's an ambitious girl. Her _aim_ in life is to become a successful lawyer.

aim, willing, am, necessity

23 Brian made his money from oil. Now he lives the high _society_ life in New York.

companion, partner, society, solitude

24 Pam's very intelligent, so she has a great _advantage_ over the rest of us when we take intelligence tests.

advance, advantage, adventure, advice

25 Mary's very interesting to talk to. I had a long _conversation_ with her yesterday.

constitution, convenience, conversation, convincing

26 Shirley's very popular. She has _numerous_ friends everywhere.

nevertheless, number, numerous, several

27 Katie's accident _distressed_ her mother very much.

dismissed, distinct, distressed, district

28 Ellen's face is swollen on one side because she has a bad _toothache_.

ache tooth, teeth pain, toothache, truth ache

29 Connie's just come home from her hundredth trip abroad. She's a very experienced _traveler_, isn't she?

passenger, passport, traveler, voyage

30 David dared to _defy_ the giant, Goliath. In the end, he won the fight.

defend, defy, differ, dive

51

PART 4 — 5 Words in Sentences

31 Sally wanted to pretend that she wasn't the one who had broken the lamp, but her _conscience_ wouldn't let her.
concerning, concert, conquest, conscience

32 Alice was in pain after her accident, so the doctor gave her an _injection_ to stop it.
indignation, information, injection, intention

33 Rosie was naughty, so her teacher sent her to the _principal_ of the school.
principal, prison, overhead, manager

34 Jane went for a swim, and _meanwhile_ Paul helped the children to collect shells on the beach.
man, meaning, meanwhile, while

35 Helen wouldn't give Peter his ball back, so he took it from her by _force_.
hard, force, power, strong

36 Modern ships are much stronger than older ones, because they are made of _steel_.
state, steal, steel, still

37 Mr. Jones is the new _Minister_ of Education in the government.
Minister, Minority, Mischief, Mr.

38 Mrs. Williams's husband died in 1963, so she's been a _widow_ for about twenty years.
girl, lady, widow, window

39 My English students have a _vocabulary_ of about a thousand words.
luxury, valuable, vocabulary, voice

40 My grandfather's so old that he can't remember our names any more. .... Yes, my grandmother's losing her _memory_ too.
member, memory, mention, remember

41 My meeting with the bank manager was very _fruitful_. He agreed to lend me the money I need.
flutter, fruitful, full, funeral

42 Hello, Rob. This is just a _personal_ call. It has nothing to do with business.
principal, personal, practical, precious

43 New York is a hundred miles from here, and our house is fifty miles, so it's _halfway_ from here to New York.
half a road, halfway, twice the way, partly

44 No beer or wine for me, thank you. I never touch _alcohol_.
acre, alcohol, aloud, although

45 No, I don't like that scarf. I like the colors, but I don't like the _design_.
design, desire, disguise, sign

52

5 Words in Sentences PART 4

46 Now that all Mary's children have left
home, she often feels _lonely_
along, lonely, long, only

47 Helen's all right. She isn't very clever,
but nobody's _perfect_
perfect, permit, profit,
purchase

48 We had a quarrel, I know. But let's
just _forgive_ and forget.
forbid, forgive, give, sorry

49 The _circumstances_ of Mrs. Carson's death were
strange. We think she may have been
murdered.
circulars, circumstances,
combinations, conveniences

50 One pound is about 454 _grams_.
1 pound = 454 g
grains, grams, kilograms,
grins

51 The club is run by a _committee_ elected by
the members.
comfortable, command,
committee, compliments

52 Our company is owned by three _partners_.
Each one has an equal share.
parcels, pardons, partners,
patterns

53 The carpet was quite bright when we
bought it, but it's _faded_ a lot now
because of the sun.
faded, failed, fated, veiled

54 One of the bears at the zoo had a baby
yesterday. .... What _sex_ is it? ....
Male.
sack, sake, sex, six

55 The local hospital is very good, and all
the _staff_ are very kind and friendly.
personal, staff, starve, stuff

56 Our teacher is a very kind man, even
though he looks very _stern_
steer, stem, stern, storm

57 Our students are making good
progress. Now when you ask them a
question in English, they answer quite
readily.
rarely, readily, recently, ready

58 The Governor called together a _council_ of
experts to deal with the problem.
candle, council, count,
county

59 Peter goes camping with the Boy _Scouts_
every summer.
Scolds, Scouts, Seconds,
Shouts

60 Ben _neglected_ his work too much, and he
soon lost his job.
disappeared, displeased,
narrowed, neglected

61 Max invited Sally to the party, but her
mother wasn't _willing_ to let her go.
permitting, pleasing,
wheeling, willing

male organ (男性の生殖器)

62 Peter's a good musician. He plays the ___organ___ in our church every Sunday.

argue, organ, original, orphan

63 Bill's a good farmer. He studied _agriculture_ at college.

agreeable, agriculture, alcohol, application

64 Peter's lazy. He never makes an ___effort___ to help his mother in the house.

affect, effect, effort, elect

65 Jim's all right. It was just a ___minor___ accident.

major, minor, minute, mirror

66 Ben seems very strong. He lifts those weights without any _apparent_ effort.

apart, apparent, appeal, appearance

67 Peter was nearly drowned when he went swimming in a place which he had been ___warned___ was dangerous.

cared, distinguished, wakened, warned

68 Jack was sick last night. I heard him _groaning_ in bed.

glowing, granting, groaning, grounding

69 Our hosts were very kind. They wined and ___dined___ us every night.

diary, died, dined, dinner

70 Pork is the ___flesh___ of a pig.

flash, flesh, fresh, skin

6 Prepositions/Adverbial Particles

6 Prepositions and Adverbial Particles

Complete these sentences with the correct word from the column on the right:

1 Are you in favor _of_ the new committee's suggestions?

of, on, to, with

2 You must do more training if you want to be fit _for_ the game on Saturday.

for, on, to, toward

3 Please help me to fold these sheets _up_ and put them away.

about, down, to, up

4 Don't you make a fool _of_ me! I know what you're doing!

at, from, of, with

5 _In_ general, our students are very intelligent.

By, In, On, With

6 We have about thirty guests a day in our restaurant _on_ average.

at, for, in, on

7 In some countries there are armed men _on_ guard at the doors of all banks.

at, by, in, on

8 Joe Smith was found guilty _of_ robbing a bank.

at, in, of, to

9 I'm writing to you _in_ haste to tell you that Sally's had her baby.

at, in, on, under

10 We're holding a big dinner tomorrow _in_(1) honor _of_(2) George.

(1) at, for, in, on
(2) for, of, to, with

11 John won his first tennis match _with_ ease.

at, by, on, with

12 You're _in_ a very good humor today!

at, in, on, with

13 What Tony thinks about this business is _of_ no importance at all.

for, of, on, with

14 I think this wine is inferior _to_ ours.

at, on, to, under

15 Teachers' behavior has an influence _on_ their students.

at, on, over, to

16 I insist _on_ my students coming to class regularly.

at, on, to, for

17 We play a lot of games—football and tennis, _for_ instance.

as, for, in, with

18 Are you interested _in_ old furniture?

for, in, on, with

55

19 If you're _in_ doubt about where to
have lunch, try the Chinese restaurant
over there.

at, in, on, under

20 Small children are often jealous _of_
the baby of the family.

for, from, of, to

21 Yes, Sally went to the party _without_
telling her parents, and they were very
angry.

from, out of, outside,
without

22 When I saw Mrs. Parker's terrible new
hat, I burst _into_ laughter.

in, into, on, on to

23 _By_ the way, could you tell me your
name again?

By, From, Out of, With

24 We have built a hospital _in_(1)
memory _of_(2) Martin Luther King.

(1) at, for, in, on
(2) for, from, of, with

25 The poor sailors prayed to God to
have mercy _on_ their souls in the
terrible storm.

for, on, over, with

· in favor of
· be fit for
· make a fool of (me)
· guilty of
· in haste
· in honor of
· in memory of
· be in a good humor
· (he) inferior to
· insist on
· for instance
· jealous of
· have mercy on

56

PART 5

1 Pictures

Look at the pictures and complete the sentences with the correct word from the parentheses:

1

This man is a _tailor_ (tail, tailor, terrible, trail). He is _frowning_ (flaming, foaming, framing, frowning) as he looks at the _seam_ (same, scream, seam, seem) of a skirt, which he is opening with a pair of _scissor_ (scholars, scissors, shivers, soldiers). The _mailman_ (letter man, mailman, male man, mail) has just pushed some letters and cards in, and they are falling on the _rug_ (rage, ragged, rock, rug) in front of the door.

2

This is a bathroom. A small girl has just brushed her teeth, and now she is _dipping_ (dipping, diving, tipping, typing) her _toothbrush_ (brush tooth, teeth brush, toothbrush, tooth buzz) in a glass of water. She is ____ (choking, spitting, spotting, supporting) in the sink. Under the sink you can see the pipe that goes to the ____ (delaying, drain, drill, drum). The girl's mother is washing her baby in a small ____ (but, pond, pool, tub) on the left. The baby is ____ (creeping, gliding, greeting, gripping) a toy.

57

3

In this room, there is a baby's _____ (climb, sleep, crazy, crib) in the corner, and a _____ (cabbage, capable, capture, carpet) on the floor. On the table there is a white _____ (cloth table, table clock, tablecloth, table cross), and on the sofa there are two _____ (curses, cushions, customers, kitchens). There is a _____ (self, shallow, shelf, shell) on the wall at the back, with a _____ (grass, mill, minor, mirror) on it.

4

This is a doctor's _____ (wait, waiting room, waiter's room, white room) in a hot country. There is a big _____ (fan, farm, fence, van) in the ceiling. The _____ (scratch, such, swing, switch) is on the wall. On the left there is a boy with a _____ (bound, round, wind, wound) on his left arm. His mother has put some _____ (gauze, oppression, relief, medicine) on it. The poor man on the right is a _____ (climate, cripple, cradle, crooked). He lost a leg in an accident.

5

This is an English "pub." Behind the bar, you can see bottles, glasses, and two wooden _____ (batteries, barrels, baskets, pitchers). Nearer us, the man on the right is holding a _____ (walking stick, walk stick, working stick, work stick) and smoking a _____ (cigarette, cinema, circular, signal). His friend is lighting his _____ (pepper, pipe, proper, purple). His can of _____ (leaves, tailor, tobacco, toothache) is open. Its _____ (laid, lead, lid, rid) is lying beside it, and there is an empty _____ (box match, matches, matchbox, much box) on the other side.

58

6

This is a store at night. The ____ storekeeper (shop copper, storeman, store copper, storekeeper) locked it at 5:30, but a robber (lover, rival, robber, rubber) has just come in, and he is planning to rub (love, rob, rub, steal) the store. He is crawling (cheering, clapping, crashing, crawling) to a drawer (draw, drawer, drawing, dwarf) which he intends to open with the blade (blade, bleed, blood, breed) of his knife. 下拿(等)

7

This is a courtroom (cart room, caught, cord, courtroom). The judge (church, judge, judgment, jug) is on the right. A lawyer (laughter, lawyer, leather, lover) is standing with his back to us, and the prisoner (poisonous, prisoner, prize man, prosperous) is sitting on his left. He has been brought here from jail (the reserve, preserving, jail, the treasure).

8

This is a swimming pool (sunning pool, swimming pool, swimming pull, water pond). There are two swimmers (bathes, summers, swimmers, swings) in it, and another is taking a shower (shave, shiver, show, shower) on the left. The water is spraying (praying, spilling, spitting, spraying) over him from above. A man is sprinkling (spinning, springing, sprinkling, *洒* throwing) water on the grass, and a boy 秋千 is on the swing (sing, swamp, swim, swing) on the right. 游泳池 游泳的人

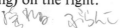

PART 5 | 2 Synonyms

2 Synonyms

Put a circle around the word or words on the right which mean about the same as the word on the left. (If more than one answer is correct, mark *all* the correct ones.)

1 opportunity *chance* — chance, change, enemy, leaving out
2 otherwise *or* — clever, cleverly, if, or
3 ought to *should* — away, must, owed, should
4 overcome *beat / overthrow* — beat, cross, join, overthrow
5 owing to *because of* — because of, belonging, borrow, lending
6 peaceful *quiet* — broken, quiet, small, strange
7 peculiar *odd / strange* — calm, jar, quiet, strange
8 plain *simple* — ache, simple, sport, not beautiful
9 powerful *strong* — dusty, half empty, poor, strong
10 precious *expensive / valuable* — expensive, priests, pushing, valuable
11 preserve *keep the peace* — earlier, keep, offer, suggest
12 pride *vanity* — acted, preached, vain, vanity 骄傲，自负的
13 problem *difficulty (n.)* — difficulty, land, likely, owner
14 proper *correct* — correct, guard, owner, suggest
15 propose *suggest* — argue, own, rich, suggest
16 provide *supply* — gain, not public, show, supply
17 purchase *buy* — buy, convince, reason, run after
18 rapid *fast / quick* — fast, hit, mad, quick
19 rare *scarce* — back, scarce, throw, true
20 rate *speed* — mouse, shake, speed, tool
21 refuse *reject* — make fresh, make happy, make less, reject
22 regret *sorrow* — be happy, know, refuse, sorrow
23 rejoice *be glad* — be glad, be sad, make less, refuse
24 remedy *cure* — be sorry, cure, far, rest
25 repair *fix* — be sorry, fix, go back, talk about

60

3 Opposites

Put a circle around the word or words on the right which have about the opposite meaning of the word on the left. (If more than one answer is correct, mark *all* the correct ones.)

1 native ~foreign~ army, artistic, foreign, good
2 naughty ~good~ foreign, good, many, much
3 neighboring ~distant~ distant, distinct, impossible, taking away
4 newly ~a long time ago~ a long time ago, niece, often, sometimes
5 northern ~southern~ both, either, southern, western
6 numerous ~few~ count, few, flew, small
7 ordinary copy, peculiar, remarkable, unusual
8 original ~copy~ copy, occasional, peculiar, personal
9 outdoors ~indoors~ entire, entrances, indoors, windows
10 particular ~general~ complete, enemy, general, special
11 patient ~impatient~ enemy, hurry, impatient, owing
12 personal ~official~ affection, effect, offense, official
13 please ~displease~ display, displease, distance, pull
14 possible ~impossible~ firm, free, impossible, nowhere
15 presence ~absence~ absence, cheap, real, refuses
16 prevent ~allow~ allow, attack, let, public
17 private ~public~ allow, enemy, public, refuse
18 prose ~verse~ evil, know, refuse, verse ~poetry~ 韻文
19 punishment ~reward~ residence, reward, sacrifice, sale
20 pure ~impure~ 不純 empty, impure, push, rich
21 ragged ~smart~ flat, happy, hurried, smart きちんとした
22 rapid ~slow~ 急速な hit, jumped, slow, smart
23 raw ~cooked~ climb, cooked, crime, crooked
24 reader ~writer~ bluer, less ready, right, writer
25 reasonable ~foolish/stupid~ a long time ago, fool, foolish, stupid

4 Derivatives

Complete these sentences with words which have the same root as the word in *italics*:

1 Our dining room is quite *wide*, but I don't know its exact __width__.

2 Our house is *surrounded* by beautiful woods, but the __surroundings__ of Jack's house are rather ugly.

3 Our ship was not far from the *shore*, so we could go __ashore__ whenever we liked.

4 With all those *attractive* dancers, our show is getting a lot of attention. It was a big __attraction__ in San Francisco too.

5 Julius Caesar returned to Rome *victorious*, having won several great __victories__.

6 Peter's an *ambitious* boy. His great __(a.) ambition__ is to become a lawyer.

7 Joe's the most *ignorant* person I've ever met. .... Yes, his __ignorance__ is terrible.

8 *Obedience* is very important in a dog, so you must start teaching Rover to __obey__ immediately.

9 Peter's been studying *magic* for years. .... Yes, he's a good __magician__, isn't he?

10 Ted's *sales* are the best in our company. .... Yes, I thought he'd make a good __salesman__.

11 Martin *suffered* a lot from pain in his back, but his __suffering__ was ended by an operation.

12 Please be *patient*! .... I'm sorry, I'm running out of __patience__.

13 Ted *possesses* certain qualities the __possession__ of which always seems to lead to success.

14 That farmer is *cruel* to his cows. I hate __cruelty__ to animals.

15 That's an *interesting* idea, and Henry's __interested__ in it too. .... If it really __interests__ you, I can tell you more about it.

16 The actors got a lot of *laughs*. In fact, the __laughter__ was almost continuous.

17 The baby was *poisoned* by something it drank. One should never leave anything __poisonous (a.)__ where children can reach it.

18 The children were *disappointed* when rain stopped their game, but their __disappointment__ did not last long.

19 The dogs were *pursuing* a rabbit, but the __pursuit (chase)__ ended suddenly when it went down a hole.

20 The *editor* of our newspaper decides on __editorial__ policy himself.

62

4 Derivatives PART 5

21 The man *confessed* to the police that he had stolen the money, and they made him sign a ___ *confession*.

22 The man who is giving the *commands* is the *commander* ___ of the whole force.

23 In the old days samurai in Japan were very concerned about their *honor*. They tried to be *honorable* ___ at all times.

24 There is a *circle* in the middle of the park, with a *circular* ___ road around it.

25 There isn't any *sand* on this beach, but the next one's quite *sandy* ___.

26 The *religion* of Saudi Arabia is Islam, and the people there are very *religious* ___

27 There's a strong *wind* today, but it isn't as *windy* ___ as yesterday.

28 The Roman *Empire* lasted hundreds of years and was ruled by many *Emperor* ___

29 Many Third World countries are *developing* new industries. But this kind of *development* ___ takes a lot of time and money.

30 These trees *grow* very slowly. .... Oh? I was wondering about their slow *growth* ___.

31 He said his property *extends* to the river, but I don't know to what *extent* ___ you can believe him.

32 They say that Columbus *discovered* America, but some people put its *discovery* ___ much earlier than his time.

33 They're going to *construct* a new hotel here. The *construction* ___ should take about two years.

34 Mexico is becoming more *prosperous*, and its *prosperity* ___ is largely based on oil.

35 This matter doesn't *concern* my department. We only deal with matters *concerning* ___ money.

36 This cable *refers* to Mrs. Jones, but I can't find any *reference* ___ to her in my papers.

37 Those books are very *expensive*, I know, but you should spare no *expense* ___ where the education of your children is concerned.

38 Very few people *remained* in the city after the fighting. And a lot of the *remaining* ___ people starved or died of disease.

39 We are *dividing* the land up among us, but its *division* ___ into equal parts is difficult.

40 We had an *exciting* time yesterday. .... Well it didn't *excite* ___ me much. I don't like that kind of *excitement* ___

5 Words in Sentences

Complete these sentences with the correct word from the column on the right:

1 Professor Jones is a famous _scholar_, and he has written a lot of important books.

collar, color, scatter, scholar

2 Queen Elizabeth the Second is the head of the British _royal_ family.

real, rival, royal, rural

3 Someone's coming! I can hear _footsteps_ on the path behind us.

feet steps, footballs, footprints, footsteps

4 Sometimes we go shopping in town, but usually we buy the things we need at the _local_ stores.

here, local, location, nearly

5 A judge must try to be fair and make sure _justice_ is done.

jealous, judgment, juice, justice

6 That bread isn't too expensive. That's the _standard_ price for a loaf.

absolute, stand, standard, strengthen

7 That dog is too young to leave alone in the house. It'll _howl_ till you come home.

hall, hold, howl, whole

8 That dress is very pretty, but it _fits_ you badly over the shoulders.

feast, feet, fits, goes

9 That man has spent half his life in prison. As soon as he's let out, he _commits_ another crime and is caught again.

commits, committees, connnects, makes

10 That man said some terrible things to me. …. He _insulted_ me, too.

increased, insisted, instructed, insulted

11 That rug will fade if you let too much _sunlight_ get to it.

sunlight, sun right, sunrise, surround

12 Was John honest? The question _arose_ when he suddenly started to spend a lot of money.

arose, around, arrows, rose

13 The animals in the zoo are _fed_ at the right time by their _keepers_.

captures, careers, carpets, keepers

14 The appointment of another doctor to help me has _relieved_ me of a lot of work.

reduced, relieved, reserved, revealed

5 Words in Sentences

PART 5

15 A trading company offers a good _career_ for young men who want to travel.
career, carriage, carry, collar

16 The Changing of the Guard outside Buckingham Palace is a very interesting, old British _ceremony_
centimeter, centimetre, ceremony, settlement

17 The big store in town will be getting its new _stock_ of summer dresses this afternoon.
sock, stalk, state, stock

18 The company John works for is very generous. In addition to a good _salary_, they give him a big car.
ceremony, salary, solitary, wage

19 The court found Frank _guilty_ of stealing the money and sent him to prison.
glide, glitter, guide, guilty

20 The day before Christmas is called Christmas _Eve_
Day, Eve, Even, Evening

21 The earthquake made all the houses _tremble_ and shake.
flutter, glitter, shock, tremble

22 The laws of the United States are based on a written _constitution_
constitution, consumption, construction, instructor

23 The King spoke before the _masses_
masks, masses, moist, most

24 The meat we get from pigs is called _pork_
park, paw, pork, port

25 The President is going to _appeal_ on television for money to help the victims of the floods.
appeal, appear, apple, apply

26 The newspapers, radio, and television are often called "the _media_
means, media, medium, midday

27 The official head of a town is the _mayor_
major, mayor, mere, more

28 The sale of oil is an important _element_ of our business.
election, element, eraser, excellent

29 There are a lot of ants in our house, and I don't know how to get _rid_ of them.
away, lid, read, rid

30 There are no buildings and no farm lands between us and the sea. It's all _wilderness_
location, lodging, wild, wilderness

1 pound = 16 ounces

31 There are sixteen _ounces_ in a pound.
an ounce of

answers, anxious, ounces, upwards

32 There are still some _tribes_ in New Guinea which have never seen a white man.

countries, nations, tribes, trips

33 Some people have so little conscience that they can't _distinguish_ between right and wrong.

distant, distinct, distinguish district

34 There aren't many people with blue eyes in Greece. The _majority_ have dark eyes.

major, majority, minority, more

35 There's only one orange left, but we can _share_ it between us, half each.

share, shave, shell, swear

36 There's really no _mystery_ about what happened to Ellen last night. She went home early. That's why you didn't see her.

minority, mist, mostly, mystery

37 There was no news about the game in the first _edition_ of the newspaper this morning, but there was in later ones.

addition, admission, edition, editor

38 There was some lightning an hour ago, but I didn't hear any _thunder_.

clouds, flashes, thinner, thunder

39 These paints can be dangerous because they _contain_ lead.

certain, contain, contest, continue

40 These sheets are expensive because they're top _quality_.

continent, quality, quantity, quarrel

41 Tim's not a genius, but he works hard and is making _steady_ progress.

instead, steady, sticky, study

42 These shoes are too small. They _pinch_ my feet.

paint, pin, pinch, pink

43 These stockings will fit any size leg because they _stretch_.

draw, pull, stretch, strict

44 Earth is just one of the _planets_ that circle the sun.

planets, plans, plants, stars

45 Our teachers are interested in the students' health and general _welfare_.

commission, construction, settlement, welfare

46 The water isn't too cold. Come on! Jump in! Don't be a _coward_.

card, cared, covered, coward

66

47 The wind's getting very strong. It's almost a _gale_ already.

breeze, gale, girl, goal

48 This dress is so expensive because it's made of the finest _silk_.

sick, silk, silly, skill

49 This is the end of the road. If you want to go any _further_ you have to do it on foot.

father, far, fur, farther

50 I'm going to write this letter out again. This is only the first _draft_.

draft, drag, draw, drawer

51 This medicine tastes nasty, but if you _swallow_ it quickly, it isn't too bad.

show, swallow, swear, swell

52 This pin is about twenty-five _millimeters_ long.

meets, meters, metres, millimeters

53 A pen like this usually costs $10, but they only _charged_ me $8 for it.

changed, charged, charmed, shared

54 This pot looks red because it's made of _copper_.

brass, cape, copper, cupboard

55 This rain just doesn't stop! It's been raining _continuously_ for the past two hours.

commonly, additionally, continuously, conveniently

56 That saddle is made of _leather_, isn't it?

leader, leather, lesser, rather

57 This town is growing fast. .... Yes, the _population_ is nearly a quarter of a million now.

popular, population, property, publication

58 This stove uses coal and other kinds of solid _fuel_.

fire, fuel, full, fur

59 To buy our house, my friend, George, lent us money on very generous _terms_.

associations, terms, times, treatments

60 To finish his work in time, John had to _sacrifice_ his usual Sunday game of golf.

sacred, sacrifice, satisfy, surface

61 Until yesterday, Jim wasn't sure how long his job would last, but then his position was made _permanent_.

perfect, permanent, perpetual, punishment

62 Are you old enough to _vote_ in elections yet?

fill, judge, separate, vote

63 We're about to sign a _contract_ with the government for the construction of a new dam.

concert, contract, control, correct

PART 5 | 5 Words in Sentences

64 We're studying hard in _preparation_ for the exams.
    preparation, pronunciation, protection, publication

65 We believe that in every mortal body lives an immortal _soul_
    soil, solve, soul, sour

66 We can offer you three drinks—beer, wine and _whisky_
    whisky, whisper, whistle, windy

67 We don't have to go out to get our newspaper. We have it _delivered_
    delicious, delivered, described, discovered

68 They found most of the stolen gold, but a _considerable_ amount had disappeared completely.
    concert, considerable, continue, many

69 There was an interesting meeting last night. The main _speaker_ was a young artist.
    speak, speaker, spider, saying

70 Our team's the best! Our nearest _rival_ is the team from the next town.
    real, rival, royal, rural

71 The main _contest_ tonight will be between Joe Grimm and the World Champion, Jesse Jones.
    concert, content, contest, continent

72 We have a lot of factories around here. It's one of the big centers of _industry_ in the state.
    indoors, industrious, industry, interesting

73 We've decided to go to Boston by train, because we're not in _favor_ of flying when the weather's so bad.
    famous, fancy, favor, vapor

74 We have to leave early tomorrow morning, so I'm going to _pack_ my bags tonight.
    back, fill, pack, peck

75 We have a vase of flowers but no other _ornament_ above the fireplace in our living room.
    amazement, apartment, astonishment, ornament

6 Prepositions and Adverbial Particles

Complete these sentences with the correct word from the column on the right:

1 You musn't get off the train while it's still _in_ motion.

at, in, on, under

2 Do you object _to_ my smoking?

against, at, for, to

3 John eats a lot. _On_ one occasion, he ate twenty-four sandwiches.

At, By, In, On

4 George is trying to get elected to the committee _in_ (1) opposition _to_ (2) old Sam Slade.

(1) at, for, in, on
(2) on, onto, to, with

5 Owing _to_ the weather, we can't play baseball today.

at, for, from, to

6 We're _in_ a difficult position. What shall we do?

in, inside, on, under

7 They're cutting the grass _for_ the game on Saturday.

by, for, towards, with

8 The prizes will be given _in_ (1) the presence _of_ (2) the parents.

(1) at, by, in, under
(2) from, of, out of, with

9 The man got into our house _under_ (1) the pretense _of_ (2) being a repairman.

(1) at, by, under, on
(2) as, for, of, with

10 You can't prevent Betty _from_ going out at night now. She's too old for that.

for, from, of, with

11 We take pride _in_ the flowers we grow.

in, of, on, over

12 We'd better discuss this _in_ private.

at, by, in, on

13 Do they provide students _with_ soap and towels here?

for, on, to, with

14 Poor Peter has run _into_ debt. He owes the store nearly $100.

in, into, on, onto

15 _To_ my delight, the children are coming to see us on Saturday!

At, On, To, With

16 That wasn't an accident! Dan broke that cup _on_ purpose.

by, for, from, on

17 The police started immediately _in_ (1) pursuit _of_ (2) the car.

(1) at, for, in, to
(2) by, from, of, with

PART 5 **6 Prepositions/Adverbial Particles**

18 It's cold today, but _at_ least it isn't raining. at, by, in, on

19 Did Mr. Gray refer _to_ us in his speech? at, in, on, to

20 Now, _with_ (1) reference _to_ (2) the plans for the new office, we're free to go ahead. (1) for, of, out of, with (2) at, on, to, towards

21 Will you please remind Helen _of_ her appointment with the dentist? at, of, on, to

22 _As_ (1) a result _of_ (2) the bad weather, the game has been canceled. (1) As, For, Under, With (2) by, from, of, to

23 After losing the first game, we got our revenge _on_ the Dragons by beating them easily the second time. from, of, on, out of

24 Someone has robbed us _of_ all our jewelry. from, of, to, with

25 You can cross _in_ perfect safety now. The bridge has been repaired. at, in, on, under

· in opposition of
· In the presence of
· under the pretence of
· in private
- To one's delight
· in pursuit of
· refer to
· with reference to
- revenge on
· in perfect safety

70

PART 6

Pictures

Look at the pictures and complete the sentences with the correct word from the parentheses:

1

This girl is a ___ *typist* (trip girl, type, type girl, typist). She is holding an ___ *envelope* (enclose, envelope, envy, involve) in her hand. There is an ___ *eraser* (area, arise, election, eraser) near the typewriter. Behind her there is a ___ *globe* (globe, glow, glue, growth) on the desk, and an ___ *atlas* (address, atlas, attach, eternal) is open at a map of Japan behind it. There is a picture in a ___ *frame* (flame, frame, freedom, frown) on the wall.

atlas (地図帳)

eraser インケビ ゴムふ 黒板ふき (duster)

2

This car has been driving along a ___ *highway* (high street, highway, hillside, way), but it has come off to fill up with ___ *gasoline* (oil, gasoline, baggage, water) from one of the ___ *pumps* (pants, pumps, purples, tanks) at this ___ *service* (gas house, service station, station, service). There is a small ___ *shed* (sad, said, shade, shed) on the right, and a man is coming out of it, holding a ___ *broom* (blame, bomb, brim, broom) in one hand, and a ___ *bucket* (backward, baker, box, bucket) in the other.

broom

shed 物置小屋

71

3

This car has been coming down a steep
~~hillside~~ (heel side, hell side, hillside, hill
and going too fast around a _bend_
(band, bend, transportation, landscape),
and it has ~~crashed~~ (clapped, cracked,
crashed, crawled) into a _brick_ (brake,
brass, brick, bucket) wall. Luckily, the
driver blew his _horn_ (harm, horn, hum,
hunt) in time for the boys to get out of
the way.

blow horn (吹哨)

4

This man has had an _operation_ (operation,
opinion, opposition, oppression) on his
stomach (astonish, stomach, stomach ache,
stubborn). You can see the long _scar_
(car, scar, score, star). He is also having
trouble with his _joints_ (bends, choice,
joints, joins). The doctor is examining
one of his _elbows_ (air bows, argues,
elbows, ill bows), and he has a bandage
around his _knee_ (need, niece, knee, knit).

5

The boy's mother is holding his _chin_
(chin, grin, joint, shine), and the doctor
is looking down his _throat_ (fruit, neck,
throat, trust). The poor boy's mouth is
open so wide that his _jaws_ (cheers, jams,
jars, jaws) hurt! The small boy's brother
is _sucking_ (shocking, sucking, suggesting,
swallowing) his _thumb_ (sum, thumb,
thunder, tomb). There is a picture of a
human _brain_ (brain, mind, mine,
thought) on the wall.

6

This man is a ____ (draft, dwarf, giant, tiny). He has ____ (cars, cures, curls, twists) all over his head. He is ____ (happy, having, hoping, hopping) about on his ____ (toast, toes, too, twos) and ____ (closing, whispering, winking, winning) at the audience. He has a sash around his ____ (visa, waist, wait, west), and bells on his ____ (heels, heirs, hells, hills).

7

This man is a ____ (baker, bargain, beggar, bigger). He is ____ (asking, begging, baking, bagging) at the side of a big ____ (deadly place, reverence, cave, tomb). There is a brass ____ (pipe, rail, rare, real) around it. A woman dressed in black is going to give him a ____ (chin, coin, colony, money). It is not a pleasant day today. ____ (Fog, Four, Fox, Hook) is beginning to cover everything.

8

On the left there is a ____ (bay, cap, cape, head). It ends in a ____ (chief, cliff, creep, steep), and the coast below is very ____ (ragged, rock, rocky, rusty). The ____ (image, right, beam, lightning) of light from the lighthouse warns ships of the danger. A ____ (fury, gale, blue, jail) is blowing, and ____ (fro, whisper, force, foam) from the waves is flying over this small ____ (ship, sailboat, sailor, sale). The ____ (card, cart, cord, court) that holds the sail has been pulled loose by the strong wind. ____ (Violence, Thorough, Flashes, Thunder) is roaring, and we can see ____ (lighter, lightning, likely, liking) near the ____ (horizon, horror, distant, cliff).

PART 6 2 Synonyms

2 Synonyms

Put a circle around the word or words on the right which mean about the same as the word on the left. (If more than one answer is correct, mark *all* the correct ones.)

1 request	ask	ask, keep back, not long ago, save
2 rescue	save	be happy, honor, keep back, save
3 residence	home	feeling sorry, giving up, home, honor
4 retire	give up work	make smaller, prize, spend, give up work
5 reveal	show	be happy, belonging to a king, enemy, show
6 reward	prize	be sorry, cure, prize, show
7 route	way	bottom, cook, far, way
8 search for	look for	look for, rare, scrape, yell
9 section	part	illness, important, part, private
10 seize	catch/snatch	catch, make a noise, quantities, snatch
11 selfish	greedy	clever, greedy, important, sea food
12 serious		clever, greedy, severe, solemn
13 severe	strict	barber, cut, more than one, strict
14 silly	foolish stupid	foolish, important, solemn, stupid
15 soil	earth	earth, mind, ship, strong
16 somewhat	rather	rather, very, what, which
17 sort	kind	game, kind, king, not long
18 struggle	fight	fall, fight, kill, stiff
19 sufficient	enough	better, enough, ill, in pain
20 support	hold up	better, game, give, hold up
21 therefore	so	absent, before that place, previously, so
22 thus	so	also, although, so, these
23 track	trail	break, catch, trail, van
24 unite	join	general, join, loose, one only
25 vain	proud	cover, get less, pride, proud
26 violate	break	blue, break, very strong, winning
27 virtue	goodness	difference, goodness, strength, success
28 vision	sight	clever, passport, side, sight
29 wholly	completely	broken, completely, covered with fur, sacred
30 yell	shout	color, give up, long time, shout

74

3 Opposites

Put a circle around the word or words on the right which have about the opposite meaning of the word on the left. (If more than one answer is correct, mark *all* the correct ones.)

1 recent	*ancient*	bad, immortal, past, ancient
2 refuse	*accept*	accept, except, increase, pardon
3 regret	*rejoice*	accept, adopt, rejoice, unusual
4 regular	*irregular*	behavior, irregular, rejoice, urban
5 respect	*scorn*	cause, damage, lose, scorn
6 rural	*urban*	false, friend, slave, urban
7 safety	*danger*	danger, dangerous, displease, lost
8 scold	*praise*	admire, hot, lost, praise
9 secret	*open*	bold, evil, let go, open
10 separate	*combined*	combined, drop, lower, whole
11 severe	*slight*	loose, lose, one, slight
12 shallow	*deep*	bright, deep, sun, won't
13 silence	*noise*	clever, married, noise, noisy
14 similar	*different*	cunning, different, difficult, harder
15 single	*married*	cunning, married, playmate, wise
16 slightly	*very*	much, too, ugly, very
17 sour	*sweet*	body, sink, sweet, without pain
18 splendid	*terrible*	kept back, not broken, saved, terrible
19 sunny	*shady*	daughter, moon, Saturday, shady
20 sunrise	*sunset*	calm, quiet, shade, sunset
21 tender	*tough*	camp, stop, tongue, tough
22 upright	*lying down*	down left, downstairs, downwards, lying down
23 useless	*useful*	urge, use, useful, young
24 violate	*obey*	gentle, obey, object, red
25 wicked	*good*	good, refused, slept, strong

75

PART 6 — 4 Derivatives

4 Derivatives

Complete these sentences with words which have the same root as the word in *italics*:

1 We have to *entertain* a lot of people, so our bill for _____ every month is high.

2 We have *various* kinds of paper, and a _____ of envelopes.

3 We *pretended* as long as we could, but we finally gave up all _____ of enjoying the food.

4 That was a *foolish* thing to say. Now everyone will think you're a _____.

5 *Appearances* aren't everything. Sarah _____ to be unpleasant, but she's really very nice.

6 What are you *waiting* for? .... I'm _____ a call from the office.

7 How *silent* it is tonight! You can almost hear the _____.

8 There was a *violent* fight in school the other day. There must be no more _____ like that.

9 There's nothing to compare with the *glory* of a beautiful sunset! .... Yes, it's _____, isn't it?

10 What does this factory *produce*? .... Here's a list of our _____.

11 What's the *difference* between all these radios? .... Well, they _____ a lot in price and quality.

12 What *value* do you place on this ring? .... I don't think it's very _____.

13 When are these students going to *graduate*? .... _____ is next week.

14 When are they going to *bury* Susan's father? .... The _____ service is tomorrow.

15 When do we *arrive* in Tokyo? .... The time of _____ is 12:15.

16 When I saw the cakes, I was *tempted* to eat some, but I didn't give in to the _____.

17 When is Mike going to *marry* Sarah? .... The _____ ceremony is planned for April 15.

18 When I was a *boy*, I lived in Canada. .... I spent my _____ in New York.

19 When I was a *child*, I really enjoyed life. .... Yes, _____ is a good time, isn't it?

20 When I was *young*, I traveled in Europe. I used to stay at _____ hostels because they were cheap.

21 When will your book be *published*? .... _____ isn't till next year.

22 When you are in *foreign* countries, remember that you are the _____.

76

23 When you see how the *poor* live in some countries, you find it hard to believe that such *poverty* can exist.

24 Where did you get this *furniture*? .... We *furnished* our house from a store in town.

25 Who did your district *elect* at the last *election*?

26 Does the *Governor* have much power? .... Not really. He only *governs* in name.

27 Who *instructed* you to do that? .... I get all my *instructions* from Mrs. Williams. 食私给信函

28 Who's your *grocer*? .... I don't know his name, but his *grocery* (is) store is called "Happy Days."

29 Who built this *engine*? .... Well, it says here that the *engineer* worked for W. Giggs and Company.

30 Who *manages* your company? .... There are about six people in top *management*, but the middle *managers* do most of the real work.

31 Who *owns* this property? .... I don't know. I haven't been able to find the *owner*

32 Who *recommended* Paul for the job in your office? .... The *recommendation* came from a friend of mine.

33 Who's going to *paint* your house? .... I've found a good *painter* for the job.

34 Who's going to *represent* our side at the meeting? 对表力 .... We've decided Tom will be our *representative* 付表)

35 Why have you put this book to one *side*? .... I put it *aside* to read later.

36 William the First *conquered* England in 1066. His victory was called the Norman *Conquest* 体胜

37 Different parts of Britain used to have their own *kings*. But now Britain is united, and it's called the United *Kingdom*.

38 Yes, John *explained* the whole thing, but I couldn't understand his *explaination*

39 On airplanes, you are allowed twenty kilograms of baggage free. If you *exceed* that, the *excess* has to be paid for.

40 You can *combine* these powders quite easily, but the _____ is dangerous. *combination*

PART 6 5 Words in Sentences

5 Words in Sentences

Complete these sentences with the correct word from the column on the right:

1 We keep our garden tidy by digging out all the _weeds_ that grow among the flowers.

hedges, planets, weeds, widows

2 We like good food, so we grow various _herbs_ in our garden.

heirs, helps, herbs, hers

3 We moved here a month ago. Our _previous_ address was 688 Elm Street.

precious, prevent, previous, provide

4 We only owe $50 to George and $20 to Helen, so our _total_ debt is $70.

all, sum, tall, total

5 We planned to spend five days in New York, but then we stayed an _extra_ day.

exceed, extend, exterior, extra

6 They don't seem to enforce the fines against littering here. Garbage is _scattered_ all along the highway.

glittered, scattered, scholar, scratched

7 We produced a lot of rice this year. The total _yield_ was much higher than last year's.

giving, outward, overthrow, yield

8 We don't like John, but ____ he's leaving tomorrow, so we don't have to see him again.

anything, anyway, anywhere, some way

9 We saw a lot of wild animals—lions and elephants, for _instance_

instance, instants, instincts, insult

10 We'll never see cheap oil again in our _lifetime_

lifetime, lively, live time, living

11 The rebels thought that their meeting was secret, but someone ____ them to the police. _betrayed_

battled, behaved, betrayed, buttered

12 France and South Korea are both _republics_

public, repentances, republics, residences

13 We usually go to church on Sunday, but if we're sick, our _priest_ comes to see us in our own home.

pleased, price, priced, priest

14 The kings and queens of Europe used to live in a very _grand_ way.

grain, gram, grand, grant

78

15 We usually shake our heads when we mean "no," and _nod_ when we mean "yes."

nod, none, not, note

16 We usually watch television in our _living room_

leading room, leaving room, live room, living room

17 We've stopped weighing things in ounces and pounds. Now we use the metric _system_.

sister, situation, stem, system

18 We went to the theater early to get good seats, because it's impossible to _reserve_ them in advance.

receipt, reserve, resort, result

19 We were having an interesting conversation, when my mother _interrupted_ us to say that lunch was ready.

entered, interrupted, trapped, undertook

20 We were hoping to get home by noon, but our plane was _delayed_

dealt, defied, delayed, delight

21 We were late getting to the party, but it wasn't our _fault_. The car broke down.

fault, force, forth, fought

22 Japan does a lot of _trade_ with the USA and Canada.

commercial, industry, trade, train

23 What are you going to eat for breakfast? .... Cold _ham_ and boiled eggs.

am, arm, ham, hand

24 What a wonderful vacation you're going to have! I _envy_ you!

enemy, envelope, envy, eve

25 What's that pot made of? .... _Clay_.

Clay, Cry, Soil, Sound

26 What's your favorite meat? .... _Beef_

Beach, Bead, Bean, Beef

27 What shall I do with these dead leaves? .... Put them on the _heap_ of leaves over there.

happy, heap, help, sheep

28 What's a trumpet made of? .... _Brass_

Bless, Brass, Breath, Brush

29 Whenever a fly came down low, the fish came to the _surface_ of the pond to try to catch it.

face, flat, race, surface

30 When George began to paint, he was _influenced_ by late-nineteenth-century French artists.

afforded, effected, influenced, informed

79

PART 6 5 Words in Sentences

31 When David died, he had no children, so his nephew was _heir_ to all his property.

air, hair, heir, her

32 When Paul decides to do something, you can't change his mind, because he's very _stubborn_

considerable, separate, stubborn, stumble

33 When I eat an egg, I always put plenty of salt and _pepper_ on it.

paper, pepper, pipe, proper

34 When I take a long walk, I always take a _spare_ pair of socks in case the ones I'm wearing get wet.

spare, spark, supply, support

35 When John's car ran into a tree and he was killed, there were no _witnesses_ to say how the accident happened.

views, visions, watches, witnesses

36 Tom's face was a picture of _dismay_ when he realized he'd left his bags in the bus station.

dismay, dismiss, mistake, undertaking

37 When my old car goes over rough roads, it _rattles_ badly.

rates, rats, rattles, restless

38 When Katie heard about her daughter's accident, it was a terrible _shock_ to her.

shake, shock, shot, sock

39 When Mrs. Jones left the party, her host _escorted_ her to the gate.

escaped, escorted, exhausted, exported

40 When our bus crashed, the driver _blamed_ the slippery road.

accused, accustomed, blamed, brained

41 When our team scores, we all _cheer_ loudly.

chair, cheer, cherry, share

42 When people are very tired, they _tend_ to get careless.

bend, lean, tend, tent

43 Now we're going to do some language _drills_

dolls, draw, drills, dull

44 When Peter lost all his money, the _disgrace_ killed him.

disgrace, disguise, displease, distance

45 When sailors want to find their position on the map, they use special _instruments_

influences, injections, instruments, insults

46 When I got *stung* by that bee, my arm *swelled* up terribly.

filled, grew, swelled, swore

47 When the police caught the man, they *twisted* his arm to make him drop his gun.

rounded, toasted, turned, twisted

48 When there is no rain in summer and the crops die, a lot of people *starve*.

famine, staff, starve, stuff

49 When the soup is nearly ready, you should *stir* a raw egg into it.

stare, start, steer, stir

50 When we came in to land at Haneda Airport, our plane passed close to *Mount* Fuji.

Moon, Mount, Mountain, Mourn

51 When we went out, it was snowing, and we were soon *shivering* with cold.

shivering, showering, sorrowing, souring

52 When we were children, we usually had to go to bed quite early, but on important days, as a special *privilege*, we could stay up till 10:00.

allow, practical, principal, privilege

53 Different countries sometimes *exchange* information on secret matters to help each other.

accent, excess, exchange, excuse

54 When you pay your bill, you should add a *tip* for the waiter.

charity, tap, tempt, tip

55 When you see a cripple, you should be kind to him. Never *mock* him.

joke, laugh, mix, mock

56 When you've finished reading that letter, please put it in the *file* marked "Travel."

fail, file, fill, fire

57 When Yuki left for San Francisco, she thought she was saying goodbye to Japan *forever*.

foreigner, forever, former, for never

58 Where can I find the names of my new students? .... There's a *list* on your desk.

least, list, rest, table

59 While I was sitting in the garden, I had a strange *feeling* that someone was watching me.

feel, feeling, firing, following

5 Words in Sentences

60 While Ben was plowing his fields, he found some buried _____, which included a lot of old gold coins.
pleasure, treasure, wealth, welfare

61 While she was going upstairs, Mary's grandmother _____ and nearly fell.
scattered, sprinkled, studied, stumbled

62 Who's in charge here? .... Mr. Davidson over there. He's the _____ of Education.
Declare, Direct, Director, Discover

63 Why's the building shaking? .... It's all right. It's only a small _____. We have lots in Tokyo.
earring, earthquake, earth wake, elephant

64 The government needs more money, so we will all have to pay more _____
expenses, takes, taxes, texts

65 Would you like a slice of _____ cake?
character, chocolate, cigarette, classmate

66 Flying kites is a traditional New Year _____ in Japan.
passage, passport, pass time, pastime

67 Joan's parents died when she was two, so she's an _____
offend, often, organ, orphan

68 Roger may be an important man in the government, but nobody could really call him a wise _____.
polish man, state man, statesman, station

69 You can wait here, and in the _____ I'll go and buy the food.
main, main time, meaning, meantime

70 You can't expect Mary to behave like a mature woman! She's a _____ child!
but, mere, more, nearly

71 You can't get wine or beer in this restaurant, because it doesn't have a _____ license.
licking, like, likely, liquor

72 Don't ask your father for money just now. He's in a bad _____
mood, moon, mouth, move

73 You know that Bill is rich, but do you know that the _____ of his wealth is oil?
sauce, source, space, spice

74 Your brother's or sister's son is your _____
aunt, niece, nephew, cousin

75 You have a toothache? Well, I have a lot of _____. I often get them, too.
feel, similar, sympathy, system

6 Prepositions and Adverbial Particles

Complete these sentences with the correct word from the column on the right.

1 For (1) the sake of (2) your parents, you should work hard at your studies.
(1) At, For, Out of, With
(2) from, of, to, towards

2 There's a lot of fruit for sale in the market now.
at, for, in, to

3 Are you satisfied with your new bicycle?
at, from, of, with

4 We grow tobacco on a small scale only.
at, in, on, with

5 I'm searching for my pen. I dropped it somewhere here.
at, for, to, towards

6 These monkeys are rather similar to ones I kept in Indonesia.
as, for, to, with

7 Don't lie on the ground. It's cold and damp.
above, on, over, to

8 Judgment has been given in our favor.
at, in, on, to

9 I was walking home last night, when all of a sudden a dog attacked me.
from, of, to, with

10 Do you suffer from lack of sleep?
from, of, off, out of

11 I think this hotel is superior to our usual one, don't you?
from, of, over, to

12 Can you supply me with eggs every week?
of, on, to, with

13 Don't shout at your brother like that! He didn't mean to kick you.
at, for, on, towards

14 Now don't get into a temper! Nobody's harming you.
for, into, onto, with

15 That violin sounds terrible! It isn't in tune.
at, in, on, to

16 We tried to stop the water, but in vain.
at, in, on, with

17 These stamps are of no value at all because they're damaged.
for, of, on, with

18 I opened the door without any difficulty.
beside, out of, outside, without

83

19 They sell bananas _by_ weight.   at, by, to, with

20 We finally yielded _to_ our friends'   from, of, to, with
   requests.

21 Everybody suffers from colds _to_   at, on, to, with
   some degree.

22 Now _with_ (1) regard _to_ (2) what you   (1) from, of, to, with
   were saying just now, I think you are   (2) by, of, to, with
   right.

23 We must get rid _of_ these mice, or   from, of, to, with
   they'll eat all our corn.   _mouse (pl)_

24 Who did you vote _for_ in the student   to, for, by, under
   council election?

25 Captain Jones has a hundred men _under_ by, on, under, with
   his command.

- get rid of
- with regard to
- suffer from
- in vain
- get into a temper
- be superior to
- in favor
- on a small scale
- for the sake of

Word List

This word list contains all the words practiced in *Word Power 3000*. In addition to the new items, this list includes all those words presented in *Word Power 1500* and reused here. (The latter are marked with (*1500*).)

Some entries are practiced in more than one grammatical form. For example *calm* is used both as a verb and as an adjective, and *load* is tested both as a noun and a verb.

Note that forms more common in British English are shown inset below the American forms if they do not also exist commonly in American English.

able	affection	application	attack (*1500*)
aboard	afford	apply	attempt
about (*1500*)	afraid (*1500*)	appoint	attention
above (*1500*)	agreeable	appointment	attitude
absence	agriculture	approve	attract
absent (*1500*)	ahead	apron	attraction
absolute	aim	arch	attractive
accent	alcohol	area	audience
accept (*1500*)	alike	argue	authority
according (to)	allow (*1500*)	arise	avenue
accustomed (to)	aloud	armor	average
ache	also (*1500*)	armour	await
acre	altogether	arrange	awaken
action (*1500*)	amaze	arrangement	ax
active	amazement	arrest	axe
act	ambition	arrival	
actor	ambitious	arrive	baby (*1500*)
actress	amount	arrow	backward
actual	amuse	art (*1500*)	bacon
add (*1500*)	anchor	article	baker
addition	ancient	artist	balance
additional	anger	artistic	balloon
admiration	angle	as (*1500*)	band
admire	angry (*1500*)	ashamed	bank (*1500*)
admission	annual	ashes	banker
admit	anxiety	ashore	banknote
adopt	anxious	aside	bare
advance	anyway	ask (*1500*)	bargain
advantage	apart	association	bark
adventure	apparent	astonish	barrel
advice	appeal	astonishment	battery
advise (*1500*)	appear (*1500*)	at (*1500*)	base
affair	appearance	atlas	basin
affect	appetite	attach	bay

85

bead
beam
beat (*1500*)
beautiful (*1500*)
beauty
because (*1500*)
beef
beer
beggar
begin (*1500*)
behave
behavior
 behaviour
behind (*1500*)
being
belief
believe (*1500*)
bend
beneath
berry
besides
betray
between (*1500*)
beyond
birth
blade
blame
bleed
bless
blessing
block
blood (*1500*)
blush
boarding
boast
bold
bomb
border
bother
bound
boundary
boy (*1500*)
boyhood
brain
brass
brave
breadth
break (*1500*)
breath
breathe
breed
breeze
brick
brief
bright

broad
broom
bubble
bucket
bull
bundle
bureau
burial
burst
bury
bus stop
buy (*1500*)
buzz
by (*1500*)

cabbage
calm
canal
candidate
capable
cape
capture
career
carpet
carve
cash
castle
catch (*1500*)
cave
center (*1500*)
 centre
centimeter
 centimetre
central
ceremony
certain
champion
chance (*1500*)
channel
character
charge
charity
charm
chatter
check
 cheque
cheer
child (*1500*)
childhood
chin
chocolate
choice
choke
choose (*1500*)
cigarette

circle (*1500*)
circular
circumstance
civil
claim
clap
clay
clear (*1500*)
cliff
climate
coarse
coin
cold (*1500*)
collect (*1500*)
collection
colony
column
combination
combine
comfort
comfortable (*1500*)
command
commander
commence
commercial
commission
commit
committee
common
companion
compare
complain
complaint
complete
compliment
conceal
concern
concerning
condemn
condition
confess
confession
connect
conquer
conquest
conscience
consider
considerable
constitution
construct
construction
consult
consume
consumption
contain

content
contest
continent
continual
continuous
contract
control
convenience
convenient
conversation
convince
cooked
cookie
 biscuit
copper
copy (*1500*)
cord
correct (*1500*)
cottage
council
county
courtroom
covered
coward
crab
crack
crash
crawl
crazy
cream
creature
creep
crib
crime
cripple
crooked
crop
cruel
cruelty
crumb
cuff
cultivate
cunning
cure (*1500*)
curiosity
curious
curl
current
curse
cushion
customer
cycle

dam
danger (*1500*)

dare	difference	due	exact
dark (1500)	different (1500)	dull	examine
darken	difficult	dumb	example
darkness	difficulty	dwarf	exceed
daylight	dig		excellent
deadly	dine	eager	excess
deaf	dip	earn	exchange
dealer	direct	earnest	exhausted
death	direction	earring	excite
debt	director	earth (1500)	excitement
decay	dirt	earthly	exciting
deceive	dirty (1500)	earthquake	exist
decide	disagreeable	ease	existence
deck	disappear	eastern	expect (1500)
declare	disappoint	edge	expense
deed	disappointment	edition	expensive (1500)
deep	discover (1500)	editor	experience
deer	discovery	editorial	expert
defeat	disease	education	explain
defense	disgrace	effect	explanation
defence	disguise	effort	export
defend	dismay	elbow	express
defy	dismiss	elect	extend
degree	display	election	extent
delay	displease	electric (1500)	exterior
delicate	distant	electricity	extra
delicious	distinct	element	extraordinary
delight	distinguish	elsewhere	extreme
delightful	distress	emperor	
deliver	district	empire	fact
demand	disturb	employ	fade
deny	ditch	employee	faint
department	dive	employer	faith
depend	divide	enclose	faithful
deposit	division	encourage	false
depth	dock	endless	fame
describe	domestic	energy	famous (1500)
description	donate	engine (1500)	familiar
desert	donkey	engineer (1500)	famine
deserve	dot	enormous	fan
design	doubt	enough (1500)	fancy
desire	dough	entertain	fashion
despair	downward(s)	entertainment	fast (1500)
desperate	draft	enthusiastic	fasten
despise	drag	enthusiasm	fatal
destroy	drain	entire	fate
destruction	draw	envelope	fault
determine	drawer	envy	favor
develop	dreadful	eraser	favour
development	drill	escape	favorable
Devil	drip	escort	favourable
devote	drug	eternal	favorite
devotion	drum	eve	favourite
diamond	drunk	evident	fear
differ	dry	evil	fearful

87

feast	funeral	grow	horizon
feather	fur	growth	horn
feeling	furious	guard	horrible
female	furnace	guide	horror
festival	furnish	guilty	horseman
fever	furniture (*1500*)		household
few (*1500*)	further	halfway	however (*1500*)
fierce	fury	halt	howl
fight (*1500*)		ham	huge
figure	gain	handbag	hum
file	gale	handful	human
final	gap	handle	humble
fine (*1500*)	gardener	handsome	humor
firm (*1500*)	gauze	happiness	humour
fit (*1500*)	gasoline	happy	hunger
fix (*1500*)	petrol	harm	hungry
flame	general	harsh	hunt
flash	generation	haste	hunter
flatter	generous	hasty	hurry (*1500*)
flesh	genius	hate	hurt (*1500*)
flood	gentle (*1500*)	hatred	hut
flutter	gift	hay	
foam	give up	headache	icy
fog	glad (*1500*)	heap	ignorance
fold	glide	heaven	ignorant
folly	glitter	heavenly	illness (*1500*)
fool	globe	heavy	image
foolish (*1500*)	gloomy	hedge	imagination
footstep	glorious	heel	imagine
for (*1500*)	glory	height	immature
forbid	glow	heir	immediate
force	glue	hell	immortal
foreign (*1500*)	good (*1500*)	help (*1500*)	impatient
foreigner	good-natured	herb	import
forever	goodness	here (*1500*)	important (*1500*)
forgive	goods	hereafter	importance
former	govern	heroic	impossible
formerly	governor	hide (*1500*)	improve
fortunate	grace	high (*1500*)	improvement
fortune	gradual	highland	impure
forward (*1500*)	graduate	highway	in (*1500*)
foul	graduation	hillside	increase
frame	grain	hinder	include
free (*1500*)	gram	hint	independence
freedom	grand	hire	independent
freeze	greedy	hold (up)	indicate
frequent	greet	hole	indignant
friend (*1500*)	greeting	hollow	indignation
friendship	grieve	holy	indoors (*1500*)
from (*1500*)	grin	home	industrious
from now on	grind	honor	industry
frown	grip	honour	infant
fruitful	groan	honorable	inferior
fuel	grocer	honourable	infinite
fully	grocery	hop	influence

88

inform
information
inhabit
inhabitant
injection
inner
inquire
  enquire
inquiry
  enquiry
insist
instance
instant
instruct
instruction
instrument
insult
intelligence
intelligent
intend
intention
interest
interested
interesting (1500)
interior
interrupt
into
involve
inward(s)
irregular

jail
jam
jar (1500)
jaw
jealous
jealousy
jewel
jewelry
  jewellery
join (1500)
joint
joy (1500)
joyful
judge
judgment
  judgement
juice
justice

keen
keep (1500)
keeper
kilogram
kilometer
  kilometre

kind (1500)
kindness
king (1500)
kingdom
kiss
knee
knot
know (1500)
knowledge

lack
landscape
large (1500)
last (1500)
laugh (1500)
laughter
lawyer
lead (1500)
leather
leave (out)
length
let (1500)
level
liberal
liberty
license
  licence
lick
lid
lie (down)
lifetime
light (1500)
lighten
lightning
like (1500)
likely
likewise
liking
limit
liner
linger
link
liquid
liquor
list
lively
living
living room (1500)
load
loaf
local
location
lonely
long
look (1500)
loose

lord
lose (1500)
loss (1500)
loud
love (1500)
lover
loyal
loyalty
luck
lucky (1500)
lump
luxury

machine (1500)
machinery
mad
madness
magic
magician
magnificent
mailman
  postman
major
majority
make (1500)
male
manage
management
manager
mankind
manner
manufacture
marriage ceremony
married
marvel
marvelous
  marvellous
masses
master
matchbox
material
mature
mayor
meal (1500)
meantime
meanwhile
measure (1500)
measurement
media
medium
meek
memory
mention
mercy
mere
merit

message
messenger
meter
  metre
method
midday
mild
military
mill
millimeter
  millimetre
minister
minor
minority
mirror
mischief
misty
moan
mock
moderate
modern
modest
moist
moisture
moment (1500)
mood
moonlight
moral
moreover
mortal
mostly
motion
motive
motorcycle
mount
mourn
movement
muddy
multiply
murder
music (1500)
musical
musician
mustache
  moustache
mutter
mutual
mystery

naked
narrow
nasty (1500)
native
naughty
navy
neat

necessity
need
neglect
neighbor (*1500*)
  neighbour
neighborhood
  neighbourhood
neighboring
  neighbouring
nephew
nevertheless
newly
niece
nil
nod
noon (*1500*)
northern
note
now (*1500*)
numerous

obedience
obey (*1500*)
object
observation
observe
observer
occasion
occasional
odd
of (*1500*)
offense
  offence
offend
official
omission
omit
on (*1500*)
onion
open (*1500*)
opening
operation
opinion
opportunity
oppose
opposition
oppress
oppression
or (*1500*)
ordinary
organ
original
ornament
orphan
otherwise

ought (to)
ounce
out (*1500*)
outdoor(s) (*1500*)
outer
outward(s)
oven
over (*1500*)
overcoat
overcome
overflow
overlook
overtake
overthrow
overwork
owing (to)
own (*1500*)
owner

pack
pain (*1500*)
paint (*1500*)
painter
pale
pan
pant
particular
part (*1500*)
partly
partner
passage
passport
pastime
patience
patient
pattern
pause
paw
pay
payment
peaceful
pearl
peck
peculiar
peel
perfect
perform
performance
permanent
personal
persuade
pinch
pious
pipe

pitcher
  jug
pity (*1500*)
place (*1500*)
plain
planet
playmate
plead
pleasant
please
plot
poison
poisonous
policy
polite (*1500*)
politeness
poor (*1500*)
popular
population
pork
porter
position
possess
possession
possible (*1500*)
poultry
poverty
powder
powerful
practical
praise (*1500*)
pray (*1500*)
prayer
preach
precious
preparation
presence
present (*1500*)
preserve
pretense
  pretence
pretend
prevent
previous
pride
priest
principal (*1500*)
prison
prisoner
private
privilege
prize
probable
problem
produce

product
professor
profit
progress
prompt
pronounce
pronunciation
proof
proper
property
propose
prose
prosperity
prosperous
protect
protection
protest
proud (*1500*)
prove
provide
public (*1500*)
publication
publish
pudding
pump
punctual
punish
punishment
purchase
pure
purple
purpose
pursue
pursuit
puzzle

quality
quantity
quarrel
quick (*1500*)
quiet (*1500*)

rage
ragged
rail
rainbow
raincoat
rank
rapid
rare (*1500*)
rare
rather (*1500*)
rattle
raw
reader

readily	ridge	semester	snake
real (*1500*)	rival	sense	snatch
realize	roast	sensible	so (*1500*)
reason (*1500*)	rob	separate	sober
reasonable	robber	serious	social
rebel	rocky	settlement	society
recent	rod	severe	soft (*1500*)
recognize	root	sex	soften
recommend	rough (*1500*)	shady	soil
recommendation	route	shame	solemn
reduce	royal	share	solid
refer	rug	sharp (*1500*)	solitary
reference	ruin	sharpen	solitude
refresh	rural	shave	solution
refuse	rust	shed	solve
regard		shelf	somewhat
regret	sack	shell	sore
regular	sacred	shelter	sorrow
reject	sacrifice	shield	sort
rejoice	sad (*1500*)	shiver	soul
relative	saddle	shock	sour
release	sadness	shore (*1500*)	source
relief	safety	short (*1500*)	southern
relieve	sailboat	should (*1500*)	sow
religion	sake	shout (*1500*)	space
religious	salary	shot	spade
remain (*1500*)	sale	show (*1500*)	spare
remaining	salesman	shower	spark
remark	sand (*1500*)	side	sparkle
remarkable	sandy	sight (*1500*)	speaker
remedy	satisfaction	silence	speed
remind	satisfactory	silent (*1500*)	spice
remote	satisfy	silk	spider
rent	sauce	silly	spin
repair	save (*1500*)	similar	spit
repent	scale	simple (*1500*)	splendid
repentance	scales	sincere	split
represent	scar	singer	spoonful
representative	scarce	single	spray
republic	scarf	situation	sprinkle
request	scatter	skilful	staff
rescue	scholar	skill	stagger
reserve	scissors	slave	stain
residence	scold	sleep (*1500*)	stalk
resign	scorn	sleepy	standard
resort	scout	sleeve	stare
respect	scrape	slice	start (*1500*)
restless	scream	slight	starve
result	seam	slim	state
retire	search	slip (*1500*)	statesman
reveal	secret	slipper	steady
revenge	secretary	slippery	steel
review	section	slope	steer
reward	seize	slow (*1500*)	stern
rid	selfish	smart	

stewardess
air hostess
sticky
stiff
stir
stock
stomach
stomachache
stop (1500)
storekeeper
straight (1500)
strait
strange (1500)
strap
strength
strengthen
stretch
strict
strip
stripe
stroke
strong (1500)
struggle
stubborn
stuff
stumble
stump
stupid (1500)
substance
successful
suck
sudden
suffer
suffering
sufficient
suggest
suggestion
sunbeam
sunlight
sunny
sunrise
sunset
superior
supply
support
sure (1500)
surface
surround
surroundings
swallow
swamp
swear
sweet
swell
swimmer

swimming pool
swing
switch
sword
sympathy
system

tablecloth
tailor
talk (1500)
tank
tax
teacup
teapot
temper
temperature
tempt
temptation
tend
tender
terms
terrible (1500)
territory
text
therefore
think about
thirst
thirsty (1500)
thorn
thought
thread
threat
threaten
threatening
throat
throughout
thumb
thunder
thus
tide
tidy
tie
tight
tip
tired (1500)
title
to (1500)
toast
tobacco
toe
together (1500)
tomb
too (1500)
toothache
toothbrush

top (1500)
total
tough
track
trade (1500)
tradition
traditional
trail
training
transfer
transport
transportation
trap
traveler
traveller
treasure
treat
treatment
tremble
trial
tribe
trick
triumph
trumpet
trouble (1500)
true (1500)
trunk
trust
try
tub
tune
twist
typist

ugly (1500)
uncertain
under (1500)
undertake
undertaking
unexpected
unfortunate
unhappy
uniform
union
unite
unload
unlucky
unusual
up (1500)
upright
upward(s)
urban
use (1500)
used to
useful (1500)

useless (1500)

vain
valuable
value
vanity
vapor
vapour
variety
various
vary
veil
verse
very (1500)
vessel
victim
victorious
victory
vigor
vigour
vigorous
violate
violence
violent
virtue
visa
vision
vocabulary
vote

wage
wages
waist
wait (for)
waiting room
waken
walking stick
wander
ward
warm (1500)
warmth
warn
washing
wax
way
weak
weakness
weapon
weave
wedding
weed
weigh (1500)
weight
welfare

western
whip
whisky
whisper
whistle
whoever
whole (1500)
wholly
wicked
wide (1500)
widow
width
wilderness
willing
wind (1500)
windy
wine
wink
wisdom
wish (1500)
with (1500)
withdraw
wither
without (1500)
witness
wonderful (1500)
wood
wooden
woods
work (1500)
worker
worm
worth
wound
wrap
wreck
writer

yawn
yell
yield
young (1500)
youth